SIMPLY THE BEST

DUNFERMLINE ATHLETIC GREATS

Foreword by Bob Crampsey

JOHN DONALD PUBLISHERS LTD
EDINBURGH

ACKNOWLEDGEMENTS

In memory of Norrie.

A special thanks to Laura Lomasney for the long hours she spent typing immaculately and deciphering my handwriting; and to Inveralmond Community High School, Livingston, for all their secretarial help.

I am indebted to all the busy people who took time to be interviewed by me in the course of the preparation of this book.

I also wish to express my gratitude to: Dunfermline Athletic FC and Chairman Roy Woodrow, Duncan Simpson and the Pars programme, the *Dunfermline Press*, *The Courier*, Graham Spiers and *Scotland on Sunday*, John Hunter, Peter Campbell, Bob Crampsey, Joe Meldrum, Dave Dawson, Tom Best, Tony Leszczuk, Pete Smith, Alex Fawcett, the Reference Department of Dunfermline Public Library; and to my family who managed without me in the summer of 1996.

The author and the publishers are indebted to *The Evening Telegraph & Sporting Post* (D.C. Thomson & Co., Ltd.) for permission to reproduce seven pictures of football actions, on pages 58, 77, 94, 97, 101, 116

Dunfermline Athletic F.C. are grateful to the Bank of Scotland for their sponsorship

ISBN 0 85976 448 6

A catalogue record of this book is available from the British Library.

Typeset by WestKey Ltd, Falmouth, Cornwall.
Printed in Great Britain by Bell & Bain Ltd., Glasgow

FOREWORD

They were nowhere, in Scottish League terms they made up the numbers, until the early 1960s, that is. Then suddenly, from being a side that had never remotely threatened, they were at Hampden three times in seven years, twice successfully and better still, became a side to be taken seriously in European football. Just once they were within touching distance of the First Division flag, the real First Division that is.

As a young reporter, I thought that for five years East End Park was almost the most exciting of my destinations. If my over-riding memory, inevitably, is of Jock Stein massively and silently for the most part persuading the Valencia officials that their side should play on a concrete surface, there are other abiding vignettes which I carry to this day. They would include admiration for the elegance of the young Bert Paton, Charlie Dickson taking advantage of a Frank Haffey blunder and Pat Gardner in the 1968 Scottish Cup Final. After all, anyone can win the Scottish Cup once...but twice?

And finally, the marvellous atmosphere created when Jim Leishman re-invigorated the club and reclaimed it from the depths of the Second Division and the collective courage that enabled the Pars to fight off the depression of two near misses and thus, eventually, attain promotion. You have to taste the salt tears of defeat to appreciate the joys of victory. John has a story to relate here that is worth the telling.

Bob Crampsey

CONTENTS

—1—

THE INTRODUCTION

On 21st March 1981 Dunfermline Athletic were playing a bread and butter league match at Firs Park, Falkirk against lowly East Stirlingshire. The Pars were a pathetic 12th in the 1st division, the 'Toy Town' league, in the words of Martin O'Neill MP. The attendance of 588 did not include one dog (you always have at least one dog at such games) which seemed to realise that the Fife club was coming off a run of five consecutive league defeats and, therefore, spent the second half looking away from such action as there was on the pitch. Even with school teacher cum player Sandy McNaughton in the team, the club's top goalscorer with 20 goals, the match ended 0–0. The club was not yet at rock bottom. Two years later they would be relegated ignominiously to Division 2 where in 1984 they would finish in 9th place. However, that March day my brother Peter and I wondered was this really the club which had won the Scottish Cup in 1961 and 1968 culminating in a European Cup Winners Cup semi-final place in 1969, represented Scotland on 5 occasions in the FAIRS Cup now the UEFA Cup as recently as 1970, played in a League Cup Final, had an illustrious history in the Scottish league, seen one player, Andy Wilson, capped 12 times, and played to average 5 figure gates at East End? In their marvellous book on the halcyon days of the club's success in the 1960s *Black and White Magic* by Jim Paterson and Douglas Scott (1984) they hoped that the services of a magician could conjure up a future of further glory for the club. Watching matches with such little atmosphere that American astronauts could have trained for a moonshot at them, the comment seemed overly optimistic yet it was almost a prophecy. Dunfermline had a new manager at the helm, the bard of Lochgelly himself, one Jim Leishman. The club was about to be revived in a way that those who supported the team in the 1970s and early 1980s could not have imagined. Perhaps the greatest tribute to big Jim is that he stopped the Pars fans living in the past. Today they look to the future with confidence. If the ambitious Board at East End have their way, the Athletic will go into the new millennium as an established Premier Division club with an all seated stadium to equal any other provincial club in the country, on a sound financial footing and again challenging in Europe.

This book is designed to be a celebration of the 1996 Championship year, which has laid the foundations for such a grand design. It reflects the contribution of 'Mr Dunfermline', Norrie McCathie, who on the field of play did more than anyone to revive the club he loved. And it focuses on some of the Dunfermline Greats since the 1960s who have become part of the folklore at this well loved club. Written by a Dunfermline supporter for those who support the club and have its best interests at heart, it is biased, passionate and nostalgic. True Dunfermline fans have all three qualities too. They needed them to survive all the grim days when the club was going nowhere, but only when you have suffered setbacks and disappointments can you truly savour the taste of success. Scotland is a nation of communities and Dunfermline Athletic is at the heart of its community. Without that relationship the club would falter and it is no accident that the club's recent revival has come about with Fifers, who are former players, at the helm. When 13,200 acclaimed the Championship triumph on 4th May 1996, the team was guided by Bert Paton, both manager and Pars supporter. Like Jim Leishman before him, Bert has learned that if the club has the legions of black and white scarved supporters behind him, they have no reason to fear anyone!

It is a sentiment echoed by Millwall manager, Jimmy Nicholl, a player with a World Cup pedigree. When a player of his class, who played at the highest level with giants Manchester United and Rangers says that Dunfermline Athletic have real potential you sit up and take notice. There were two reasons why he came to East End as a player. First he felt he'd become a coach prematurely at Ibrox and second 'those astonishing crowds'. 'In 1989–1990 we were averaging a remarkable 11,000' he recalls. 'It might not seem a lot compared to say Old Trafford but the volume of noise produced at packed compact East End was worth the proverbial extra man. The highlights of my career were the games at all levels when my team won against the odds and there were plenty such games with Dunfermline'.

This book then is not about some small provincial football club. In the Premier League Dunfermline Athletic's 5 figure gates can only be surpassed, on a regular basis, by five clubs. Outwith the Premier, they have always had the greatest drawing power as evidenced in January 1987 when the Athletic, a Division 1 team just out of Division 2, played before 16,500 at Easter Road in the 3rd round of the Cup. 7,000 clicked through the turnstiles at the Pars' end for a match described by Alex Ferguson as 'the tie of the round'. The BBC cameras were also there and the atmosphere did nothing to weaken the suggestion that the club would be an asset in the newly talked about Super League. Leishman, meanwhile, declared 'Oh Lord I'll tell ye nae mair fibs; If ye'll only let me beat the Hibs'. The Pars lost 2–0 but big Jim was convinced that a sleeping giant was stirring and manager and supporters were off on a crusade.

Norrie McCathie told me that 'Dunfermline was Scotland's Newcastle'. It was not just the strip he was referring to, it was a reference to the loyalty of local people to the club. It is a loyalty rewarded by a Board which always charges the minimum it can for stand seats eg in 1996–97 a terracing ticket of £10 compared to just £11 for the wing stand. The immediate area has 70,000 inhabitants and, with average crowds exceeding 10,000, it means there is no club in the country which has a larger support as a ratio of the population. To put it in context, Rangers would have to attract an average gate of 100,000 to compete yet they draw from all over the UK! Why then does Dunfermline attract crowds that Falkirk, St Johnstone, Raith Rovers, Motherwell, Kilmarnock, Dundee etc can only dream of? Part of the answer may be tradition. Those who became hooked on a Saturday afternoon in the 1960s and witnessed the Cup Finals of 1961, 1965 and 1968, the great European nights when the saltire flew proudly over the old stand have, for the most part, stayed. It may be success. Perhaps half the Pars legions were in nappies or weren't even around as the Cup was paraded to the tune of Cliff

Richard's 'Congratulations' in April 1968, but they've witnessed the 1st division Championships of 1989 and 1996, 2nd division Championship of 1986, the Youth Cup Victory 1988 and Scottish League Cup Final appearance 1991. However, I suspect it is the family atmosphere at the club and the relationship with the local community generally. Part of the role of being Pars manager is to foster that relationship, to get out and about and publicise the club and to attend functions both for the fans and local community. You see evidence of this over the years. Jim Leishman took the team to BBC's 'Pebble Mill At One' to publicise the 'East Enders' pop record and he then organised 'The Centenary Club' the popular private club for the club's supporters which contributes much needed finance to the club while giving members the chance of a major prize, discounts at local stores, functions, holidays, the excellent tours of the stadium taken by Peter Campbell which are always in demand, coaching sessions for the children etc. Bert Paton and Dick Campbell have carried on the tradition, speaking to as many fans at the Centenary Club and Supporters Club functions as they can and thinking nothing of the sacrifice in giving up considerable chunks of their own free time. They are rewarded then, not just by the large numbers who want to get involved in the club but by the large proportion of women and children who attend regularly. The Athletic were one of the first clubs to have a 'ball girl' or female mascot at games, to have a parent-and-child gate, female toilets and modern catering facilities. The crowd is sporting, well behaved and extremely knowledgeable and, on a Saturday, there are vast numbers wearing the familiar black and white colours in the shops and in the local parks. Unlike the experience in so many towns of comparable size, you do not see convoys of coaches heading off to support the big city clubs. The locals head to East End Park or spend the afternoon not too far from a radio awaiting word that the heroes in black and white have done it again.

However, Dunfermline did not always play in black and white! The club, formed in 1885 as a breakaway from the local cricket club only 18 years after football began as a serious sport in Scotland, actually played in maroon tops and blue shorts according to teacher John Hunter in his definitive *Dunfermline Athletic 1885–1985*. He found that the club was founded at a meeting at the Old Inn on Tuesday 2nd June 1885 and that East End Park was leased from the North British Railway Company a few days later. Hunter points out that timing and location were crucial factors in getting Dunfermline established. More and more of the industrial workers in the mines, factories and mills were gaining a half day holiday on a Saturday and attending the football match became a cheap regular form of entertainment. Wages were rising, transport was cheap and TV was many years away. The coming of the Forth Railway bridge in 1890 and the Rosyth Dockyard in the Great War would cut journey times to major population centres like Edinburgh while adding the potential of thousands of new supporters. Veteran fan Alex Fawcett of Rosyth points out that this is how the name 'Pars' came about. While many argue that it is an abbreviation for 'Paralytics' the hardly endearing chant of the supporters in the 1950s when Dunfermline were a yo yo team up and down to Division 1 but visibly more at ease in the second; it came about much earlier when Rosyth sailors from Plymouth carried banners to games with 'Plymouth Argyle Rosyth Supporters' emblazoned on them. I wish I could be given a fish supper for the number of times I have been asked that by supporters at an away ground!

At the front of any 'Pars Programme' you find the club's first honours, ie, the Scottish Qualifying Cup of 1912 and Central League Champions 1911, 1912. (In fact their first real success was winning the Fife Cup in 1887.) It is a feature of provincial club's programmes, of course, that among the honours are listed the runners up spot or semi final appearances. Dunfermline are no different, the Scottish League Cup Final appearance of 1991–92 rates a proud mention. You are also reminded that the club's highest position in the Scottish Football League was 3rd in both 1965 and 1969. However, these were real triumphs for the club before the Great War. Football was still quaint. Football historian Bob Crampsey has pointed out in *The Scottish Football League, The First Hundred Years* (1990) that it was not unknown for a team to be a man short, where upon a spectator would be chosen from the crowd or even a player volunteered from the opposing team! John Hunter found that the Athletic would sometimes abandon an away game early if it was obviously beyond saving and catch the last train home! On another occasion an away team did not turn up so the Pars kicked off, scored and claimed the win. The clubs match commentator for the blind, Joe Meldrum, recalls post-war matches where a ref could still congratulate a goal scorer! More often than not, the *Dunfermline Press* implored the fans not to turn against the team when they sustained defeats and local churches condemned the riots which were not uncommon in this period. Dunfermline were denied a place in Divisions 1 or 2 where they would have been along side such giants in the league as Cowdenbeath, East Stirlingshire and Dumbarton. That was why winning the prestigious Qualifying Cup rates a mention in the programme even today. In 1912 Dunfermline were allowed to join Division 2. It was to be the dawn of a new era as they were to wear the familiar black and white stripes for the first time. The league was suspended during the Great War and the ground commandeered by the army. By the 1920s the public was desperate to return to normality and football, the dance hall and the cinema remained the working man's hobbies and for that matter women too. The *Dunfermline Press* recorded that the Pars were playing to huge gates, a large proportion of the crowd was female and yet the club could not survive on gate receipts alone, all features we would recognise today.

Today the club depends on everything from shirt sponsorship to corporate hospitality to supplement gate income; in the 1920s music hall acts helped raise finance for the club as did Scotland's first ever supporters club. This was the period when the club sensationally signed Andy Wilson, the Ally McCoist of the 1920s. The ex Hearts player would win 6 caps while at East End and scored over 100 goals in the process. He was long gone by the time the Programme proudly tells us the club won their first ever Championship in 1926. The star player of the period was now Bobby Skinner, a player lethal in front of goal, as his 127 goals testify. He was very sharp and fast by the standards of the day though John Hunter reminds us that the offside law was more favourable to strikers then. The club could not have won the league at a better time, the overdraft was huge and local derbies of 20,000 plus against rivals Cowdenbeath were sorely missed when they gained promotion first. Much worse was to follow when Rosyth Dockyard was shut down against the backdrop of the Depression. The *Dunfermline Press* recorded that Dunfermline began the innovation of charging less for the unemployed. In the 1930s the club languished mainly in Division 2, fending off financial crises, dependent on its supporter's clubs for ground improvements and with the Board asking for league reconstruction. In the 1920s the *Dunfermline Press* had spectators asking did the club really want promotion?

As the Second World War began it was believed that all football at East End would cease due to the proximity to Rosyth naval base. However, the authorities relented and crowds complete with gas masks could watch the depleted team carry on in friendlies and informal tournaments until, as Polish war historian Tony Leszczuk points out, the Polish army occupied the ground briefly. John Hunter discovered that one remarkable feature of the informal league structure then was the awarding of 3 points for a win. The club's most remarkable success to date came in 1949–50 when the 2nd Division team reached their first national final, the Scottish League Cup under manager Webber Lees. The team, which included Gerry Mays and Jimmy Cannon, sensationally put out Hibs in the semi-final 2–1 with Hibs reject Mays enjoying sweet revenge to turn around a 1–0 deficit with 2 goals against a team comprising Turnbull, Ormond and Reilly. Dunfermline though went down 3–0 at Hampden to high flying East Fife. In the 1950s Dunfermline became a yo yo team languishing more often than not in Division 2 before unspectacular forays into the higher league.

When former miner Jock Stein from Hamilton, a former Albion Rovers player, was appointed manager in March 1960, it is well documented that he told the media he could not wave a magic wand. The appointment by Chairman David Thomson was inspired. Stein, one of the greatest managers the world has ever seen would go on to win the 9 Championships in a row with Celtic. For Dunfermline he was like the genie of the lamp. He transformed the club from a struggling 2nd Division backwater with a stadium to match into one of the top clubs in Europe with one of the best grounds in Scotland and yet he was there barely four years. Stein was impressed by the Dunfermline players he inherited and he knew there was money to spend. He insisted on the players wearing a club uniform, of travelling in a luxurious coach, of eating at the best restaurants and he coached them as a team not as individuals. They were thoroughly briefed on the strengths and weaknesses of opposition teams. He was astute in the transfer market bringing in Willie Callaghan and Willie Cunningham among others. He also knew the club badly needed a youth policy to ensure a constant supply of young talent. While children elsewhere in Scotland sit on a grandparents knee and hear about Jack and the Beanstalk and Goldilocks and the Three Bears, Dunfermline kids, with their mothers' milk, are regaled with the story of how the Pars had to win all the remaining 6 games in the 1st division in 1960 to stay up and then how Stein masterminded the 1961 Cup Final victory. After a 0–0 draw before 113,228 fans at Hampden Dunfermline went on to beat overwhelming favourites Celtic 2–0 in the replay before another 87,660. The Cup went to the Auld Grey Toun for the first time not just because of the goals by Thomson and Charlie Dickson but because of the breathtaking display by goalkeeper Eddie Connachan who brought the Celtic forwards to their knees in disbelief! In the same year a raw teenager call Alex Edwards joined the club. In the Stein period Dunfermline became established in Division 1 but were making their name in Europe.

Jimmy McConville points out that Dunfermline Athletic were the first club in the country to charter a plane to go to a tie in Europe. They reached the last 8 of the Cup Winners Cup, had the sensational 6–6 (agg) FAIRS Cup matches with Valencia and knocked out Everton, the Bank of England team 2–1 (agg) whose manager had the temerity at the Cup draw to enquire 'Who's Dunfermline?' Dunfermline's seven years proudly representing Scotland in Europe came to an abrupt halt with the defeat by Anderlecht in 1970. The club was not only out of Europe, they were almost out of existence. Yet only a few years earlier things had seemed so rosy. Willie Cunningham the new manager took the club within an ace of a sensational Cup and league double in 1965. Today it is remembered for Kilmarnock taking it at the last gasp at Tynecastle on the last day of the season yet it is almost forgotten that Dunfermline's inexplicable 1–1 draw with lowly St Johnstone in that April allowed Killie the opportunity. In the Cup Final 108,000 watched Dunfermline in the unaccustomed role of favourites, lose a game, still regarded as one of the classics, 3–2 to Celtic. Jock Stein said later that it was this game that set Celtic up for their later triumphs. Willie Cunningham, unaccountably, left out top scorer Alex Ferguson but Melrose and McLaughlin put the Pars in the driving seat 2–1 at half time. Herriot was disappointing in goal and Melrose's belief that Dunfermline would seal it with a strong wind at their backs in the second half was not justified. Celtic's spirit and McNeill's 81st minute winner put paid to the Pars dream of their greatest ever season. A 5–1 league win over Celtic didn't matter tuppence.

The Athletic now were at their peak and in 1968 they came 4th in the league and in 1969 3rd. George Farm, the former Blackpool goalie, took them to a second Cup Final triumph in 1968 when a team including Pat Gardner, Alex Edwards, Bert Paton and Roy Barry defeated Hearts 3–1 before 56,365. En route they had outplayed and outclassed Celtic, the European Cup holders, in a 3rd round 2–0 win still regarded as one of the Pars greatest ever displays. Again it meant the open topped bus through the streets of Dunfermline and thousands ecstatically singing 'Congratulations' the Cliff Richard hit opposite the City chambers. The goalscorers Gardner (2) and Lister had both been brought by Farm from Raith Rovers. 27,816 plus thousands who broke in, attended a subsequent league match against the league champions Celtic, a record which for safety reasons will never be equalled. Former Dundee player Hugh Robertson later remarked that Scotland now had a 'big 3' ie the Old Firm and Dunfermline! One wag changed a road sign outwith the town to read 'Dunfarmline'! As Dunfermline reached their peak in losing by 1–2 (agg) the 1969 Cup Winners Cup semi-final against Slovan Bratislava and the 1960s drew to a close, no one could have anticipated the club's sudden decline. It is a myth that Dunfermline averaged huge crowds in this period. While 16,600 attended the match against Slovan in April 1969, in comparison the 1st division Championship match in May 1996, in a period when there are so many other competing attractions for a much more affluent local population, was watched by 13,183. Dunfermline now had a financial crisis of epic proportions. Years of paying huge bonuses and wages and splashing out huge sums to attract the most talented players could only be justified if there was success on the pitch. In 1971 the club's players had grown old together, there were injuries to key players, they avoided relegation by the skin of their teeth, and the fear was that the club would go the way of Third Lanark. Dunfermline did survive the crisis, thanks to a public appeal masterminded by Director Leonard Jack. Supporters and businesses gave generously and hostile take over bids were resisted. It did not save them on the pitch. Just one year later, in 1972, they returned to the 2nd division from whence they had come in 1958. Many Pars supporters look on the period till 1986, when Jim Leishman took the club back into the 1st division, much the same way as Historians regard the Dark Ages, and just as the book *1066 And All That* ends suddenly when Britain lost its place as a world power so the book *Black and White Magic* stops too. The authors concluded with Leonard Jack's famous remark that some see 'Dunfermline as a sinking ship but Dunfermline will sail again'. There was not much evidence for such optimism.

Even Jim Leishman did not bring instant success in the way Stein had. In his first season the Athletic would end up a humiliating 9th place in Division 2. In the years which followed Alex Wright, George Miller, Harry Melrose, Pat Stanton and Tom Forsyth all tried to waken the sleeping giant. Financial stringency wasn't the only problem. As Aberdeen and Dundee United were to experience in later years, the fans still regarded the initial lack of success as merely a blip in an otherwise wonderful period. Dunfermline were now a top European team. Surely they would revive? Suffice to say that one of their few successes was to come off the field when the club gained national TV exposure with Alex Wright, Jim Fraser and John Cushley winning BBC TV's popular Quiz Ball! Among the players in this period were Kenny Thomson who was to make 348 appearances between 1970 and 1982 (227 of them consecutively), Jim

Leishman, Ken Mackie and Graham Shaw. With the youngsters allied to the experience of the likes of Alex Kininmonth, George Miller took the club back to Division 1 with 95 league goals, the highest in Britain. The Athletic were desperate for cash, a situation not made easier when Mackie astonishingly turned down a transfer to Rangers. Despite a good start to season 1974–75 the Pars failed to make the cut to ensure a place in the Premier Division which was to do so much to revive Scottish football. A few years earlier a place would have been a complete formality. East End's floodlights were overhauled in preparation in for the colour TV cameras which were hardly likely to come. One year later, now with popular Harry Melrose at the helm, the Athletic were in free fall into Division 2. They remained there till 1979. Effectively they were now a Division 3 team in all but name. Some gates could be numbered in their hundreds. Part-time contracts were now the order of the day. The club had to endure playing in the qualifying rounds of the Cup (on one occasion in 1978 losing to Brechin in the process) and the club only kept their heads above water if they could sell a star player on an annual basis, such as Alan Evans who went to Aston Villa. One player who was to prove so influential in this period was Bobby Robertson. He made his debut in 1977, wore 8 different jerseys in his time at the club, and was to lead the club back to the top. Remarkably he continued all this with a career in medicine. Obviously he didn't just have brains in his head! Dunfermline's success in 1979 was largely due to Andy Rolland. The Pars fought a tremendous battle with Berwick Rangers and Falkirk, which went to the final game. An Andy Rolland penalty put the Pars up and he commented later that if he hadn't have scored he might as well have walked out of the stadium never to return!

The fact that the crowd for what is effectively a local derby exceeded 6,000 and the previous Cup tie with Hibs brought in a healthy 11,000 showed the club still had an untapped potential few clubs in Scotland could emulate. For the next 3 years the Athletic flirted with relegation with Pat Stanton as manager. Tom Forsyth replaced him and in 1983 the Athletic went down yet again. Crowds were hovering around a pitiful 2,500 yet in 1981 a mid week Cup replay would attract 9,000 and the cameras but the gallant Pars went down 1–2. Dunfermline's Board had given Pat Stanton the sort of financial backing Harry Melrose could only have dreamed of but it had all been for nothing. The merry go round of players and managers had taken its toll. In October 1983 the club appointed reserve coach Jim Leishman as manager. He was the 4th man in the post in 3 years, the appointment merited only a few lines in the national papers and big Jim thanked personally every fan who sent a card to wish him luck. The club did finish an abysmal 9th in Division 2 but on 28th January 1984 came one match which would change history. The team travelled to Ibrox and lost the Cup tie 2–1 to Rangers but had taken the lead through Rab Stewart amidst scenes of delirium. Jock Wallace the Rangers manager faced a shock bigger than Berwick 1967. Leishman said later the game was a turning point.

In 1985 they missed out on promotion by 1 point having begun the season with 6 victories on the trot. On the final day Pars fans celebrated on the pitch as a radio station gave the wrong score from rivals Alloa's match. Leishman swore that day the Athletic would never experience this disappointment again. Dunfermline Athletic historian John Hunter had hoped to complete his definitive centenary history of the club with the team's promotion. It was not to be but, as they won the Division 2 Championship in 1986 then were promoted to the Premier Division as runners up in 1987, he documented the longed for success in *Premier Bound*. The period was also covered in *Leishman's Lions* by Robert Fraser, *Scottish Football Today 2* and Leishman's own book *The Giant That Awoke* both of which I co-wrote. The books were symptomatic of the relief that Dunfermline, at last, were back where they belonged. John Watson was again top scorer, Norrie McCathie had again played in every game, over 100,000 had clicked through the turnstiles and, thanks in part to the increasing success of the fund raising Centenary Club created two years earlier, the club was on a sounder financial footing. The stadium gained a new supporters shop, facilities for the disabled, new crush barriers, family enclosures, modern stand seating, crowd control security cameras and a huge new car park though there was not enough cash yet for the badly needed new floodlighting system or under soil heating. However, the coming of the new technique of sand slitting meant fewer games called off due to heavy rain. Off the pitch big Jim had nothing to learn about public relations, the national TV coverage given to the release of the Pars theme 'East Enders' being a typical example. On the pitch he was working a successful double act with coach Gregor Abel whose record included the promotion of every club he'd been associated with. Pip Yeates was now physio and he was to be honoured by carrying out that role on a Scotland basis at Euro '96. Ian Campbell and Joe Nelson were in the back room team. The Youth Policy was also revitalised, the club winning the reserve league east in 1987 and 1993 and the Youth Cup in 1988.

In the first season in the dizzy heights of the Premier League, Dunfermline faced the difficulty that 3 teams were to be relegated to take the top division back to 10. The first home game attracted more fans than the entire gate in Leishman's first year as manager and the season is best remembered now for the sensational Cup victory over Rangers 2–0 in February 1988 and 'that' goal by Mark Smith! 104 years after the club was formed, on 13th May 1989, Dunfermline finally captured the Division 1 Championship. 12,889 watched the 1–1 draw with Meadowbank which sealed the flag. 1989–90 saw the Pars in the Premier Division and 212,211 fans attended the home games, the 5th highest in Scotland. Class players the calibre of O'Boyle, Kozma, Nicholl, and Rougvie had been attracted to the club. Dunfermline finally gained revenge over Hibs, after five consecutive Cup defeats over a decade, when they beat the Edinburgh side 1–3 at Easter Road to reach the League Cup semi-final. They also reached the Scottish Cup Quarter-Final. The Leishman era came to an end in July 1990 and a lot of the sheer fun of the period went with him.

The new manager was Iain Munro who latterly had been co-manager with Jim Leishman. In 1990–91 he helped the club consolidate in the Premier though crowds slumped alarmingly and the correspondence column of the 'Press' was full of letters demanding Leishman's return. He could not redeem himself even when his team reached the Skol Cup Final in October 1991 by which time he had been replaced by Jocky Scot and Gordon Wallace. Dunfermline's hero in this period was, undoubtedly, flamboyant goalie Andy Rhodes who came to East End at the height of the 'Leishman affair' for a bargain £80,000 from Oldham. He had played in a Littlewoods Cup Final at Wembley and his relationship with the fans and his joking were a welcome relief in a miserable period. As the team strode out at Hampden they had amassed 2 points from 13 games. They lost the lack lustre Final 2–0 to Hibernian. In May 1992 they were relegated.

Back in March 1962 an enthusiastic young player was photographed excitedly beside his new shirt in the home dressing room. A similar photo was taken of Bert Paton the day he became manager in 1993, sitting with the no. 8 jersey on the peg above his head. It was the fulfilment of his life time's ambition and he was determined from the outset to recapture his success at St Johnstone. The fans took to him immediately for he was one of their own, a hero of the 1968 Cup winning team and all those great nights in Europe. He immediately renewed the relationship with the fans and, after the desperately close things in 1994 and 1995, he finally saw his beloved club promoted to the Premier Division on 4th May 1996. He brought back Dick Campbell as coach and together they recaptured the team spirit and the fun in the way he'd been taught by Jock Stein. 13,183 fans packed into East End Park to see Andy Smith and a penalty by Marc Miller ensure the 2–1 defeat of Airdrie to pip media favourites Dundee United by 4 points. Paton had kept the club on top despite working on a shoe string budget, being forced to sell Jackie McNamara to slash the club's debt, having to cope with tragedy and a succession of injuries. Thanks to Paton, they were simply the best.

—2—

JIM LEISHMAN

In the autumn of 1983, Jim Leishman, the club's reserve team coach, was sitting beside club captain Bobby Robertson on the bus returning from a reserve match at Dumbarton. The club was at rock bottom and Jim was trying to rebuild a football career so savagely cut short as a player. Bobby Robertson, who on the pitch would lead the club back to the very top of Scottish football, was trying to give time and commitment both to his job as a junior hospital doctor and to the football club he loved. The team was stuck wretchedly near the foot of Division 2, the players' morale was shattered and there was no atmosphere at East End where only a few hundred now came to a game. They both spoke with passion as they recalled the great nights in the 1960s. They analysed why things were now so grim and, with ludicrous optimism, discussed the future. 'Leishman had big plans' recalls Bobby 'He wanted the club in Europe'. 6 weeks later, at the age of only 29, he would become Scotland's youngest manager and he must have brought a wry smile to the faces of many fans as they read his first programme. It was fine to offer honesty, enthusiasm, 100% effort and loyalty—but he was going to bring back the halcyon days of the 1960s into the bargain! This was despite the fact he would be a part time manager. Indeed, the only full timer was Sheila Peters in the office and the ground staff. Privately he was unsure how long he would survive in the manager's chair but was just delighted that he would gain a mention in the club's Centenary history.

When he left in July 1990, the 2nd Division Championship flag 1986 flew over the club, something they had not won since 1926, along with the 1st Division one for 1989, never won before. The BP Youth Cup 1988 and Scottish Reserve League Championship 1987 had nestled in the trophy cabinet. In addition Duncan Simpson of the 'Par's Programme' discovered that they were only the second club ever to go from Division 2 to the Premier in just 12 months and they won the Division 2 flag with the highest number of goals of any club in Britain. Dunfermline's reemergence in this period has, of course, been unequalled in Scotland and is an encouragement to other ambitious teams in the lower divisions. A combination of superb man management, the backing of an ambitious board, his appointment of an outstanding coach in Gregor Abel, remarkable wheeling and dealing in the transfer market, a uniquely personal relationship with the fans and the community, his accessibility to the media and the ability to get every player in a black and white jersey to give 100% were to lead to these triumphs. Whenever I spoke to Jim about these achievements, he always paid tribute to his back room staff and players. He was also in awe of the success Stein, Cunningham and Farm had brought to the club but few would deny he equalled, if not surpassed, what they attained. As the last person to interview him (for Scottish Football Today) before he was effectively brushed aside, I found the parting of the ways totally inexplicable. The club was attracting class players like Istvan Kozma, Milos Drizic, George O'Boyle and Andy Rhodes and one was left in no doubt that big Jim wasn't just thinking in terms of consolidating in the Premier Division, he wanted to see the club back in Europe too.

The outcry which followed, ranging from angry letters to the 'Press' to the march by thousands down the High Street to the ground was predictable to all but to those Alan Burnet called, in *Scottish Football Today* magazine, 'the faceless people who created the situation'. Dunfermline could now lay claim to the tag that Partick Thistle enjoy namely 'the club everyone loves'. The Leishman era, which he went on to describe in *The Giant That Awoke* (1990) was one of the happiest stories ever told in football. The attendances at East End in his final season amounted to 212,000. That was the 5th highest in Scotland. 'Who is to say where we might have ended up together' he wrote ruefully? It was a pertinent question given that when he was appointed, seven years earlier, the ground had all the atmosphere of the adjacent cemetery.

After the failure of so many predecessors to prod the sleeping

Jim putting his point to Ian Archer of S.T.V.

giant, the club needed a messiah in 1983 although Jim was always quick to point out there were 'no 3 wise men' at his birth in 1953. He was born into a close knit family which actually supported Hibs and, like most in the small community of Lochgelly, his Dad worked down the pits. However, his brother Mitchell is a Celtic fan and on one occasion, when Jim would not get him free tickets for a match against the Glasgow club, Mitchell held a banner aloft in the stand proclaiming 'Leishman must go'! Although at the age of 8 Jim had heard from excited school friends about Mr Stein winning the Cup for Dunfermline against all the odds, a fact guaranteed to make him a hero for life, there was not the money to go and watch Dunfermline, nor was there the time. His first, albeit vague, recollection of a Pars match was the thrilling 6–2 defeat of Valencia one year later but he was happier playing for the local Primary team or organising matches at the local park, as often as not playing in goal. In one such game he met up with the Campbell twins and Ian put 5 goals past him! By the mid-1960s, though, he was supporting the Athletic on a regular basis when they were at their peak. Not only did this entail walking to the game, it meant disappearing from Beith High School before the school day was over if there was a mid week European fixture! In June 1971 he signed professionally for the club he adored. He already had school boy and youth caps. The day when chief scout Andy Young asked him if he would like to sign an S Form still remains one of the proudest of his life. That was in 1968 when Dunfermline Athletic won the Cup. The stadium was among the best in Scotland and he could rub shoulders with his heroes. He thought centre half Roy Barry was the greatest of them all and was amused that other club's fans sang disparaging songs about him even when the Fife club weren't the opposition! By the time Jim made the start of season team photo in 1971, only Callaghan, Edwards, Lun, Gardner and Paton of the Cup winning team remained.

Indeed the photo is something of a collector's item now as it includes Jim and Bert, at the beginning and end of their respective playing careers. They were both to bring the coveted Division 1 Championship to East End. Jim admits now that, at the time, the club's lack of success was indeed seen as a blip. Were they not one of the top teams in Europe? Were they not able to compete with the Old Firm for wages and bonuses? Would more talented players not come in to replace the Cup winners who were growing old together? Well, actually no - the team slid down the league, there were consecutive poor seasons, no challenge for honours, gate receipts fell and the club's future now depended on youngsters like Jim coming through. Jim played 7 games that season, celebrating his first goal against Clyde in April 1972 as if he had just won the European Cup Final. When he scored again, to give the Pars a rare victory at Ibrox, it gave the club a chance to stay up. With the score at 3–3 he took the ball in the inside right position and beat 2 defenders before crashing a left foot shot past keeper Peter McLoy. Joe Meldrum, the Pars commentator for the blind, says it was definitely the best Jim ever scored. When they were subsequently relegated in a home defeat by Dundee United, he was gutted, but the remnants of the Cup team were devastated. Leishman resolved that day that he never wanted to suffer such an experience again. By 1972–73 the Cup team was gone and the new manager George Miller, who had a considerable influence in Jim, was in charge. The club went on to score the record 95 goals as Miller blended the precocious talent of the likes of Ken Mackie and Graham Shaw with the experience of Alex Kinninmonth and John Arrol. Jim was learning. George Miller was brilliant at delving in the free transfer market and arranging exchange deals. 'He also knew the psychological approach' says Jim. 'In a match on a winter's day at a packed Ochilview he had us wearing light blue tracksuit bottoms under our shorts. We took so much banter and so much stick, including wolf whistles, that we were all fired up and won 0–2. George kept the experiment going through that winter and we gained promotion though gates were now under 5,000 and we needed 12,000 to break even.' In 1973–74 it was vital that Dunfermline stayed up, as everyone knew that a Premier Division was on the way. They did by the skin of their teeth on goal difference and Jim made 40 appearances. 'The season had 2 great moments' he recalls 'Miller had brought back Jackie Sinclair for a bit of experience and no one will ever forget his goal against St Mirren. I gave him the pass on the half way line, he took a couple of strides and he unleashed an unforgettable rocket. I'll never forget a 2–2 home draw with Rangers either, Ian Campbell's corner volleyed home by Alex Kinninmonth was shown time and time again on TV that year.' Dunfermline played before 27,000 that season at Celtic Park and the Rangers game attracted some 17,000 but, off the field, a Sunday market and the creation of the Paragon club were still necessary for much needed income.

There was also a crucial Cup tie against Falkirk that season played on a Sunday due to the power cuts. Jim found one of his opponents was one Gregor Abel. Their paths were to cross again! People were beginning to remark that Jim might one day play for Scotland and he took some encouragement from the fact that Ken Mackie and full back Jim Wallace had now been rewarded with under-23 caps for their excellent season. As season 1974–75 began, everyone knew the Premier League was just one year away. The big defender would only make 3 appearances. In a mid week match, on 21st August 1974, he had a terrible collision with Hearts' Jim Jefferies. As he lay in agony, the ref' shouted at him to get up but his leg was broken in 3 places. Today he is able to joke about it. 'I called across to Dick Campbell who immediately put his stinking sweaty shinguard between my teeth - I forgot my leg instantly!' He had hundreds of cards and threw himself into a tough training schedule designed by Ralph Brand, the coach. The photos of Jim in this period show him typically clowning around with all the other crocks at the club but, in truth, he was desperately concerned there might be no way back on the pitch, a season which began so promisingly ended with 4 pathetic points from 15 games and, when Jim did play for the 2nd team, he knew he'd lost a couple of yards in speed. The following season Harry Melrose became the new manager, gates halved, 11 players had to be freed to keep the club above water and the coach was relieved of his duties. The longer the season went, the more it became apparent that relegation was more likely than promotion and this despite the brave efforts of former Pars star Harry Melrose to work on a shoe string budget. In a 3rd round Cup tie the Athletic put up a gallant effort only to go down 3–2 to Hibs. In the league they were in 2nd bottom position despite the gallant efforts of the new strike force of Ian Hall and Roddy Georgeson. On 18th February 1976 big Jim did make his long awaited comeback albeit as sub, in an easy 5–1 victory over doomed Clyde. However there was to be no miracle, Dunfermline sank even further into the mire and Jim was transferred to Cowdenbeath in a swap deal for Bobby Morrison. He was only to play 11 games for them under Frank Conner in 1976–77. 'I knew it was a big mistake as I walked around East End for the last time' he says. 'Ironically one of my last games was against the Pars there. The chant of 'reject, reject' really got to me and, as my pal Alan Evans was giving me a hard time on the pitch, I pulled his shorts down in pure devilment. I was red carded, of course.' He had played 81 full games for Dunfermline over the 5 seasons and scored 6 goals despite being a defender. An era was at an end.

In the years which followed he played for Glenrothes and Oakley, managed Kelty Hearts, became coach at Cowdenbeath under Andy Rolland, and, in July 1982, became Youth coach at East End in the Pat Stanton era. When Tom Forsyth replaced him, Jim was elevated to reserve coach. Then, in October 1983, he became manager though, surprisingly, he was not one of the 40 applicants for the post. With the club ending up 6th bottom of Division 2 that first year, there was little suggestion of the glory days to come. Such was the plight of the club, that there had to be a long Board meeting to sanction £2,300 of expenditure on Alan Forsyth's transfer from Raith Rovers, as the club was still haunted by the cost of Doug Considine from Aberdeen. There had been little return on that £43,000. However Leishman is quick to remind us that Pat Stanton did bring in the likes of Norrie McCathie, Steve Morrison, Grant Jenkins and Bobby Forrest. Other influential players of the period like Jim (Ziggy) Bowie and Bobby Robertson had been snapped up in the Melrose era. A few years later the same Board would splash out £540,000 on Istvan Kozma. Frankly, Jim was utterly depressed when he walked about East End that autumn. There was none of the buzz of the 1960s. He also knew full well the team he had inherited weren't capable of going anywhere. However, the season did see the sensational 2–1 defeat at Ibrox in which Rab Stewart astounded everyone by taking the lead. That one match, big Jim still feels, was the watershed.

Then Gregor Abel was snapped up as coach. Things were taking shape. It was still the worst season in 3 decades, however. Director Martin Sisman even asked the *Dunfermline Press* not to keep reminding its readership of the fact! There was one footnote to 1983–84. Jim had signed a red haired striker called John Watson for only £300 from Hong Kong and he only scored three goals in 18 games. Clearly he had not yet got into his stride. By 1984–85 Jim's own team was taking shape and, in a fantastic home Skol Cup match before a packed East End, the team only went down 2–3 to Celtic because of their superior fitness. The Pars were already top of the table, after winning the first six league games. Jim recalls 'I knew the lads wouldn't need motivating but I began saying daft things like - you are up against Willie McStay, aren't you glad it's not Paul, Burns is out of position, McAdam will be on the wrong foot, Reid will be attacking so he'll leave gaps at the back for you to exploit. Look, you are really only playing 7 men! Once the game began, I kept running out of the dug out in sheer excitement until 2 goal John

Watson came across and told me to calm down!' The league season proved an exciting one as the Pars battled it out with Montrose and Alloa. Like George Miller, he had to sign the best players he could on the free transfer circuit. Knowing the club desperately needed cash to bring in quality, he took on the role of commercial manager as well. He would now go around supporters clubs, pubs, social clubs, youth clubs and schools building up support. Jim was in his element. By 1985 Jim had signed goalie Ian Westwater for only £3,500 from Hearts, to eventually take over from club doctor Hugh Whyte. He had a host of schoolboy and Scottish professional caps and had the honour of being the youngest player to play in the Premier Division. Jim's faith in him was to be repaid by his numerous shutouts, his instinctive saves, acrobatic goalkeeping, his excellent organisational ability, his skill at taking a crossball and overall fitness. His role would be crucial in the Championships of 1986, 1989 and 1996. By the second last game the Athletic had to go to Alloa, who were one point ahead in 2nd place. 4000 Pars fans went on the pilgrimage to little Recreation Park, where a missed Morrison penalty and a subsequent 0–0 draw put paid to all their hopes.

In the final match at East End, thousands were to celebrate promotion on the pitch due to a radio station giving an incorrect scoreline from Alloa's match. Inside the dressing room Jim choked back the tears as he told the players the real result. The Pars in their Centenary year were doomed to stay put. Jim told the media later that he felt as though he'd won the Pools, only to discover he had not posted the coupon'! As usual the Pars' support, at 47,000, was the best outwith the Premier Division and Motherwell. That summer saw the Centenary celebrations and many of the former stars enjoyed them including winger Jimmy Tonner from the side of 1912 culminating in the match against Alex Ferguson's high flying Aberdeen which the Athletic won. Many had gone on to greater things yet they retained a great affection for the club. At the party after the match the former players watched the highlights of the 1960s on a special STV video Arthur Montford had presented, and everyone spoke to Mr Stein, of course. His biographer, radio commentator and

Scottish football historian Bob Crampsey was MC at the subsequent Centenary dinner. Almost every Scottish football club attended. It was not all looking back at the past. Jim set up the 'Centenary Club' having learned of the Bolton experience and, 10 years on, the financial help it has given the club and the relationship it has built with the 1000 supporters who are members have been considerable. East End Park in those days could turn into a First World War mud bath and in August one match was called off due to flooding! The season is remembered for a number of reasons. John Watson hit a magnificent 31 goals and won the Golden Shot Award. Stephen Morrison perfected his Rivelino free kicks. John Hunter's definitive book on the club's first 100 years was published. There were 25th anniversary Cup celebrations. There was the sad death of Jock Stein. There was the adventure of the Pebble Mill trip to publicise the record 'East Enders'. Roy Woodrow, the owner of a soft drinks company, became a director. There was considerable talk of a Super League and though few doubted that the Athletic, with their stadium, crowd potential and tradition would be invited, big Jim actually spoke out against it saying it would not be worth it if it meant the demise of community clubs such as Cowdenbeath, East Stirlingshire and Stenhousemuir. He also could not see the point of Hearts and Hibs sharing a super stadium in the capital but felt what was needed was the inclusion of population centres such as Inverness and East Kilbride and, in remarkably prophetic words, he said, back in 1986, that it would make good sense for clubs such as Clyde to relocate to a new town. Overall though, Jim wanted to see the Pars succeed on their own merit and they did. Playing each team three times they took 57 points from the 39 games and pipped Queen of the South by two points. Average home gates edged up to 3,000 and the team had 17 successive league games without defeat.

They did, however, lose their Cup tie 2–0 to Hibs before a 16,000 crowd. East End had gone wild as early as April 19th when the 4–0 defeat of East Stirling ensured promotion but the Championship duly came on the 29th in the mid week fixture at Stenhousemuir. The 0–0 draw there meant the Pars were dependent on Queen of the South drawing at Cowdenbeath but they led

1–3. As the fans moved to the exit and the players shook hands, the tannoy announcer suddenly said 'I have a score here that may be of interest. It's Cowdenbeath 3 Queen of the South 3!' The little park erupted and big Jim and John Watson were carried shoulder high to the dressing room and the champagne. The convoy back was a little reminiscent of the 1968 Cup journey and, as they returned to East End and the Paragon to celebrate, they were joined by the sporting Queen of the South team who, despite their obvious disappointment, had come to congratulate them. The Athletic were on the way back. A Championship flag had not flown over the stadium in 40 years. No one was more proud to hold the trophy aloft than captain Bobby Robertson. Jim Leishman said 'No-one was more dedicated as a player or more loyal as a fan than Bobby. From the start I told him, tongue in cheek, that I would make him the best right back since I played! In fact, he developed into the best right back I have ever seen and he deserved the Player of the Year Award. He was a great man marker, inspired all his mates and could be my only choice as club captain. He trained on his own because of his career but was always super fit. There was no Pars player you would depend on more.'

The Athletic's total home attendances were now 58,000 and that was 10,000 more than the best in Division 1! As the Division 1 season 1986–87 began, big Jim was not going to promise miracles. He wanted to consolidate their position. Among the signings was one of major significance, namely the tricky versatile left-footed powerhouse, Ian McCall from Queen's Park. The aptly named 'Diego' was signed for a mere £7,000 and, despite his asthma and short sight, he scored 8 goals in the promotion year which followed. One year later he would move to Rangers for £200,000. His form was devastating but the Athletic simply could not turn down that sort of cheque. Leishman still grimaces at the torrent of personal abuse he took at Dunfermline's next match from the Pars fans. Ian later returned to the club in 1990 saying 'The East End atmosphere was unique'. Meanwhile big Leish was telling the players, privately, that 'they should go for it'. Promotion again was not beyond them. Jim Leishman and some of the squad were now full time and, in the month that the

Jock Stein suite opened, he took a leaf out of his hero's book, kitting the players out in blazers and flannels. The club got off to a good start taking 18 points from the first quarter of 11 games but that slipped to 11 in the second quarter. It was still not easy to attract quality players with Premier experience to the club, which was still essentially part-time. The Pars best players were also being watched by bigger clubs notably John Watson by Crystal Palace and both Leish and Abel were linked with vacancies at Hibs and Aberdeen. The competition was with Morton and Dumbarton for the top 2 spots and, at Christmas, Dunfermline pulled off a crucial win 1–2 at Boghead, a game dubbed 'Clash of the Titans' by Radio Forth's John Wood. Then they drew 2–2 at Morton. As many as 4,000 Pars fans were now travelling to the away games. By the time the Pars players, wearing 2 strips to ward off the hypothermic conditions, drew the New Year match with East Fife 2–2 (with Jenkins contriving to score at both ends), the Athletic had been honoured with the news that both Watson and McCathie would play in the Scotland semi-professional team.

The club played honourably in the inevitable Cup defeat from Hibs 2–0 with 7,000 Pars fans travelling. Although, by now, a lot of fans had spent an evening watching the video of the Pars golden years, Karen Grega the 'Crocodile Dunfermline' Aussie Commercial Manageress struck a chord when she said that with such progress being made, the time had come 'to forget the 1960s'! On 25th April 1987, 5,482 watched Dunfermline snatch promotion for the first time to the Premier Division, defeating Queen of the South 1–0. They were the first Fife club to achieve it, as club Historian John Hunter had prophesied 2 years earlier. Morton took the Championship, one point clear. One week earlier the nervous Pars had lost at home 0–2 to Brechin in the worst performance of the season. A number of fans threw their scarves on the track in disgust. Jim made a point of wearing one the following week. 'I found the pressure just awful. We got an early goal through Willie Irvine then we missed two tremendous chances. Queen of the South pushed forward, pinned us back and looked more like the team going for promotion than a team flirting with relegation. I was shouting so much from the stand that Gregor Abel in the dug-out switched his walkie-talkie off! Minutes lasted hours till that whistle blew. The tension, nerves and anxiety all drained from my body within seconds. I was so relieved for the players, supporters, Directors and town. I got chucked in the bath, the champagne flowed, we all sang our heads off and photos were taken. However, we did not manage the Championship. As so often we failed in a vital match at Airdrie 2–1 then somehow lost 1–0 at Montrose, the league's poorest team and fielding trialists and a reserve keeper. However, promotion was a great achievement. We ended up with 56 points and a total home attendance of 100,000 and we were back at the very top.' Bobby Robertson said later 'I cannot put into words just how excited we all were.' As season 1987–88 began, the buzz was back at East End. Of all the signings Leish made, the most significant was Craig Robertson for £25,000 from a reluctant Raith Rovers. He would score 19 goals in his 63 appearances, a fact which did not go unnoticed. Eventually he moved on to Aberdeen for £175,000 only to return like McCall. Leish says 'Craig was one of the nicest players you could want to meet. That he ended up the Premier Division's highest scoring midfielder in a team which was struggling ahead of the likes of Paul McStay, spoke volumes for him.' Big Jim knew full well that the rewards for the club coming 4th bottom in the season, before yet another reconstruction would be immense as the Pars would effectively compete in a mini-league with Motherwell, St Mirren, Falkirk and Morton. 12,000 fans turned up for the gala occasion of the Athletic's first ever Premier match against Hibs and the shirt-sleeved crowd were rewarded with a scintillating 3–3 draw—'one of Jim's three fondest memories' of his time at the club. Big Davie Young got two of them.

In front of a capacity 18,070 crowd and the cameras the Athletic later beat Celtic 2–1 with Westwater having a blinder. However, premature talk of a place in Europe subsided as international packed Rangers came to East End and won 1–4. Those who attacked Jim for the transfer of McCall which followed should note that Souness upped the bid 3 times to £200,000. Leish later declared 'I have sold an ace to buy 4 kings' as the club signed Holt, Kirkwood, Smith and the tragic Riddell.

Dunfermline hit a succession of bad results at the same time as the players, who'd brought the club up from the 2nd Division, were disappearing. The Pars found themselves along with Morton, Falkirk and Motherwell on the deck of a sinking ship looking at one lifebelt. Leish's cavalier attacking style won the club a lot of friends but did little for the points tally. All the same, the Pars did turn it on sometimes and a 32,000 crowd saw a magnificent 2–2 draw at Ibrox.

At the turn of the year with Motherwell galloping off into the sunset and against a background of 5 consecutive league defeats, they were to be lambs to the slaughter in the 4th Round home Cup tie with Rangers. Ian St John and Jimmy Grieves gave TV publicity to Leish doing his 'David and Goliath' story to the team. There was also some poetry 'Oh Lord, You know the dangers when my players take on the Rangers; Pars 2 Gers wan - what a thought to beat that Souness man'! The game was a classic, maybe the greatest of the Leishman era. 19,360 packed into East End, £250,000 spent on the terracing having increased the capacity, with a huge media presence and Dunfermline went on to win a fast and furious game 2–0. In the opening minutes flying winger Mark Smith lofted a spectacular ball over the head of international goalie Chris Woods and then, after surviving an hour of Rangers continual onslaught, a Beedie corner was tucked in by Smith at the near post for John Watson to head spectacularly past Woods as the Rangers defence stood like statues. The subsequent Quarter-Final at Hearts was a complete anti-climax and the Athletic were outplayed 3–0. Against this was the background of 8 league games without a goal but, despite some commendable results at the end of the season including draws with the New Firm, the club went down yet again. 'We'll be back' said the banners in the final game at Celtic Park. Dunfermline had come a long way in a short space of time and they would be better prepared next time.

Jim knew, as 1988–89 began, that the Athletic were now by far the biggest club in Division 1 and every team would be gunning for them. They were full time, had the largest squad, were just out of the Premier and they were backed by the enviable Eagle Glen training facilities. All the bookies quoted the club as favourites. There was no need to add significantly to the squad though Paul Smith was snapped up from Motherwell. Leish described him as a player with a great attitude, a grafter who could play in midfield or up front and get the occasional goal. Initial results were good, the gates were up. Games in Division 1 were now televised more often, which was a real boost but a 2–1 defeat at Brockville confirmed that the main threat would come from the club's main rivals of recent years. However, a succession of draws coupled with bad injuries saw the team slide to 6th place till a 0–1 win at Perth began a run of 8 wins in 9 games. Dunfermline lost Craig Robertson but the good form continued and at Hogmanay the Pars were 1 point adrift of Falkirk with 27 points from 20 games. 12,889 saw a fabulous 3–0 victory. There was an atmosphere at such games now that even a Fife derby with Raith could no longer match. The season just got better and better as a flattering 1–3 win at New Year at Starks Park was followed by a 0–2 win at Airdrie. An outstanding 0–0 draw before 17,000 and the cameras against Aberdeen in the Cup showed the Pars were not far from Premier standard though Leish admits he did get rather carried away before the game in the dressing room. 'Remember' he told the players 'whatever you do today, you've done so well to get to this stage.' The players laughed 'What do you mean—it's our first game' they shouted back! The Pars went down 3–1 in the Pittodrie replay.

As the season wore on, alarm bells sounded after a 4–0 thrashing at Falkirk and a 0–1 home defeat by Raith. Leish felt later that maybe they should have played a defensive game in both. However it was all to work out in the end. As Falkirk had an unhappy afternoon at Airdrie the Pars pulled off a vital 0–1 win at Forfar, thanks to a superb drive by Davie Irons which beat Stewart Kennedy all ends up. On the 13th of May 1989, after failure a week earlier to wrap it up against Clyde, Dunfermline won the priceless point in the 1–1 draw with Meadowbank which gave the club their first ever Division 1 Championship. A vast amount of money had been gambled on success in one season and Jim knew that, for financial reasons there would be sackings and players allowed to go if they failed now. A crowd of 12,976 watched the jittery Pars and, as news came through that Falkirk were doing well, former Pars favourite Bobby Forrest crossed the ball for Scott to score for the Thistle. Bobby had his head in his hands and did not accept any congratulations. Then luck, which in a long season of injury and suspension had seemed conspicuous by its absence, suddenly smiled on the club. John Watson drew Jim McQueen and scored the golden goal. The Pars did not look like losing it after that, especially as news filtered through that Falkirk were now in trouble up at Forfar. Jim was given a huge plastic bottle of champagne and dashed around the track pretending to be an aeroplane. Everyone ended up in the bath and then the players, the Directors and fans began one of the biggest parties the town has ever known as they moved on from one bar to the next. 104 years after the club was founded, big Jim had given the Auld Grey Toun the 1st division flag for the first time. Fans too young to remember 1961 or 1968 savoured every minute of it.

When the flag was unfurled at the opening league game of 1989–90 that August, a lot of the Tabloids were publishing their guess for the final league positions come May and, although there were slight variations in the bottom 4, one constant was that the Athletic always came bottom. Jim used that to psyche up and anger his players. They now had that intangible quality called experience, the squad was much stronger than back in 1987 and they were no longer going to be an 'insurance policy' for other teams. The Athletic could also count on Jimmy Nicholl whose pedigree included Rangers and Manchester United and Doug Rougvie who had seen it all at Aberdeen and class act George O'Boyle from Bordeaux. Leish made it clear they were again in a mini league of Hibs, St Mirren, Motherwell and Dundee and they must learn from 1987–88 and not drop points to these clubs. Against the rest of the Division they would have to go in for what Bob Crampsey called 'damage limitation'.

As usual, the Pars won the opening league game but most unusually, after years of failure, they pulled off a sensational 1–3 Skol Cup Quarter-Final win against Hibs. They were thumped 5–0 by Rangers in the Hampden semi but underlined their ambition in signing the exciting magyar Istvan Kozma for

£540,000. By now there was some mindless talk about getting back into Europe again as results were so good, especially as they beat Celtic again at home 2–0 and actually went to the top of the league for 3 whole days after a 1–1 midweek draw with Motherwell. Ross Jack, in superb form, scored 12 goals in 16 games. Former Pars star Doug Baillie quipped 'the team finishing above the Athletic in the table will be champions'! There were heavy defeats from Aberdeen and Rangers but a crucial 1–0 win over Dundee on Boxing Day which took the club 8 points above the danger zone. The pressure was evaporating by the time the Athletic beat Celtic 0–2 on their own turf for the first time since 1968. After an atmospheric Cup victory over Cowdenbeath at neutral Raith, Dunfermline performed creditably to draw 0–0 in the Cup with Celtic at East End before being outplayed in the replay. Despite a succession of injuries and suspensions Dunfermline finished a mere 5 points adrift of a place in Europe.

Leish shows his true colours

There had been 2 great Cup runs and they had finished 8th. 212,211 had filed into East End. 'We were probably 2 years away from a place in Europe' says Leish 'but I was not to find out'. In 1996 in his first season at Livingston he took them to the Division 3 Championship. He is manager of a new football club with a magnificent all seated stadium, a large potential support from a new town population of 48,000, with the youngest average age in Scotland. Crowds are the highest, by far, outwith the top 2 divisions and the club has attracted considerable sponsorship. Someone was needed to go around the town to the schools, pubs, social clubs and youth clubs and attract the local people to Almondvale Stadium. He is going to do it with Livvy all over again. Could he return to East End Park, as manager of Livingston, in the Premier division?

—3—

BERT PATON

On Saturday, May 4th 1996, as the Athletic players prepared to go out on the pitch for the Championship match at home to Airdrie before a crowd of 13,183, manager Bert Paton had one question for the team. 'Do you want to play against the likes of Gascoigne and van Hooijdonk next season or do you want another year stuck here'? Nicknamed 'Chateau Dunfermline' by the critics, who felt the Athletic had bottled it in 1993, 1994 and 1995, earning the Flag they so desperately wanted had entailed 4 years of expectation, disappointment and frustration. However, Paton was quick to point out they lacked nothing in terms of resilience or temperament during the run in, as they'd only lost one of the 17 games. 'Everyone kept going on about Dundee United, St Johnstone and Morton' says Bert but, while we had that one defeat, we had the wonderful 0–1 victory at Tannadice, and defeated the other two at home 3–2 and 4–1 respectively. 'I honestly didn't feel under the same pressure as in 1995' he stresses 'I lost a stone in weight then but you have to remember I'd a terrible shortage of players, and in the last dozen games not one of our strikers scored. The real pressure was surely at Cappielow on 4th May, it must have been horrendous as Morton played Dundee United. This time, as the tension mounted, I would relax by having a long walk with my dogs.'

However, Paton confirms what many Pars supporters had suspected and, indeed, feared 'Yes I was ready to quit if the Pars did not gain promotion this time. If we hadn't made it, I would have found it very difficult to carry on, after the three previous failures. All I wanted was to see this club I love back at the top where they belong, and I would have stood aside to let someone else take us up.' The Board would not have heard of such a thing. It had been a traumatic season with Jackie McNamara having to go to appease the club's bankers, the tragic death of Norrie, the

A Dunfermline v Kilmarnock clash in the 1960's. Bert Paton scoring.

long injury list and as usual having to work on the sort of budget that wouldn't have kept Billy Kirkwood at Tannadice in after-shave! On the eve of the match Alex Ferguson of Manchester United, who at one time was the Athletic's most prolific scorer, phoned Bert and offered his good wishes and a few tips on how to cope with the pressure of last day nerves. 'I wasn't surprised he phoned,' says Bert 'not only is he a great friend but you find that any players who have been here retain a great affection for the club and the spirit among the players in the 1960s was brilliant. I wanted to repay the courtesy but I reckoned it would take a steadier hand than my own to dial the number after our night of celebration'! Even Paton had to admit though that there had been many matches in the 95–96 season when the team played better. 'Actually the Airdrie match was a bit of an anti-climax', Bert states, surprisingly. Club Chairman Roy Woodrow conceded, later, that when Airdrie deservedly equalised, he thought the Championship would slip through their fingers again. The team put Bert through a roller-coaster of emotions all afternoon.

The terracings were jammed with expectancy, nerves were on edge and the fans, who had been assailed with everything from Freddie Mercury to Luciano Pavarotti, seemed to freeze as the teams came out, which was hardly surprising as the news came through that United were one goal up on Morton. In the 29th minute, when Andy Smith scored, you could almost reach out and touch the relief. As the fans enjoyed the half-time entertainment, the match having kicked off 12 minutes late, there was delirium on the terraces as news came through that Morton had equalised. As the second half got under way the Pars played some dire stuff and Airdrie's delightful possession play seemed to frighten Dunfermline's wits. In the 56th minute Hetherston lofted the ball into the net but, rather than suffer another bout of the jitters, it forced the Athletic back into action. East End and Cappielow went wild together as Morton equalised at 4.37 pm. As Marc Millar, the former Brechin player, went over to the far side to take an innocuous throw in, 13,000 people suddenly erupted! Bert Paton immediately sent on the 2 subs to confirm what was obvious to everyone. Craig Robertson and Andy Tod were doing a jig in the centre circle while players hugged and shook hands with the opposition. Yet there were 12 minutes to go. The penalty which sealed the Championship was taken coolly as always by Marc Millar. 'If you are not confident, you shouldn't take it' he said later. 'Mind you, I'd had a penalty competition on the Friday with Derek Fleming and he won'! Alan Moore secured the penalty with a run in on goal and was upended by former Pars favourite Andy Rhodes. Millar slammed it into the bottom right hand corner sending Andy the wrong way. It wasn't till 5.35 that proud captain Craig Robertson could hold the Trophy aloft as the helicopter had not only been delayed in transporting it, but the pilot decided against a landing at East End. It was somehow apt that the Athletic's support should have to wait just a little longer. After all, they'd been patient for 4 years. As the Athletic's players toured the old stadium, surrounded by the media and bearing their new 'Champions' tops, Bert Paton got detached from them. Having done a host of TV and radio interviews, he was to be seen making sure all the disabled fans in front of the enclosure got to touch the trophy

The deadly trio – Paton, Fleming and Ferguson.

and then the children at the front of the terracing. There were hugs and kisses and tears. He was among his own. In the helicopter, tangerine and blue Cup ribbons lay discarded on the back seat. The story of a memorable day would go down in black and white!

When Bert Paton was signed by Jock Stein 'the greatest influence on my whole career', in July 1961, another memorable day was still being celebrated, the famous cup win a few weeks earlier. A local lad, he came from a large family in High Valley-field and, like so many local boys did a stint at Rosyth Dockyard and down the pits. At Torryburn school he lived for sport, and football in particular. He played left half in those days. 'I just knew that one day I would play for the Athletic and, in later life, I felt it was my destiny to manage the club'. With words as prophetic as those, it is no surprise he was signed by Leeds United and got turned down for the manager's job at the club when he applied in 1983. 'That was the only time I applied and I got it a decade later.' He was snapped up by Leeds having played in the Scottish Juvenile Cup Final for Tulliallan Thistle. He was to find himself in the team photo with Don Revie and Jackie Charlton. I'd been expecting to sign for the Pars but the Leeds manager drove personally to High Valleyfield to sign me!' 'The player who most impressed me as a lad was Jim Baxter, then a Raith player but with his obvious class and swagger as he played at East End I knew instantly he was cut out for greater things. I cannot pick who was my favourite while a player in the 1960s.

There were too many skilful players then but if there was one player I would have liked to have seen in a Pars strip it was AC Milan's Franco Baresi! At Leeds I was played as a centre-forward in the reserves and scored 22 goals, but the club was relegated and I was off loaded as part of the inevitable cuts in the playing staff. I was utterly devastated but, while on holiday at Butlins in Skegness, Jock Stein phoned and on 31st July I signed. I played my first game against Stirling in the March having scored regularly in the second team.' Paton was not the only bright new prospect that season. Callaghan, Lunn and Sinclair joined him in an exceptionally talented second team. The Pars were only the fourth Scottish team to play in Europe and reached the Quarter-Final of the European Cup Winners Cup. The Athletic, the only British club, went down on a 3–5 aggregate. Meanwhile, Bert scored his first league goal against League Champions Dundee —a total of four for the season. The following season is best remembered for the defeat of Everton in the Fairs Cup, the epic matches with Valencia and the opening of the magnificent new stand. Stein felt that playing in Europe was vital as it made it easier to attract youngsters to a provincial club. Alex Edwards and Tom Callaghan were the latest on this seeming conveyor belt of talent and, that December, Jock played a new attack of Bert alongside Edwards and Sinclair, talked through the game by the experienced Alex Smith and George Peebles. 'The latter was the greatest influence of all the players' Bert points outs 'You know, in recent years, George Peebles promised Dick and me and our wives a slap up meal when we won the Flag. He dodged it in 1994 and 1995. Dick and I are still waiting for the night out'! 'I got my first taste of European football with the club's tour of Norway. Of all the nations I was to visit later, I liked the Scandinavian ones best. You were well fed and so well looked after. Meanwhile, I was still playing mainly for the reserves but in those days gates would have equalled many a Division 1 game today'.

The following season Jock Stein spent a few days as a guest of Italian cracks Inter Milan as he felt that what he learned in terms of tactics and coaching he could pass on to the young players like Paton. It made it all the more of a bombshell in February 1964 when Mr Stein announced his resignation. Cunningham took over, though Stein doubted whether he could manage those with whom he'd only recently played. He brought Ferguson, McLaughlin and Kilgannon to the club. Ferguson commented that having players the calibre of Edwards, Sinclair and Paton at the club 'prompted him to sign.' It also meant that the Athletic had a plethora of forwards, prompting Dickson to leave for Queen of the South. 1964–65 was to be, arguably, the club's greatest ever season. 22 year old Paton himself had put in for a transfer yet, in November 1964, played in the defeat of Stuttgart in the Fairs Cup. The league results were outstanding, none more so than in January 1965 when Bert swept home a Ferguson cross to beat defensive league leaders Kilmarnock 1–0 and retain a 100% home record. He was rewarded with a place in the Fairs Cup Round 3 match against Bilbao. In the league it was one of the most exciting seasons ever with Kilmarnock, Hearts, Hibs, Dunfermline and Rangers all in contention. In an exciting Cup Semi-Final at Tynecastle, Dunfermline defeated Hibs 2–0 with goals from Melrose and Smith but lost crucially to them in the league 1–0 away. Hopes were raised again with a thrilling 3–1 win at home to Rangers but, unaccountably, a 1–1 draw with St Johnstone in mid-April 1965 effectively blew all Pars' hopes. A week later, Dunfermline lost the epic Cup Final to Celtic 3–2 with a team minus Ferguson, or 7 goal Bert Paton. 'That Cup Final result was my most disappointing moment ever with the club' he still says emphatically. 'I cannot believe the club took nothing from the season'. His last goal had been against Third Lanark in the February and he now required a cartilage op. The final goal scoring chart for season 1964–65 further emphasised what an outstanding season it had been with Ferguson on 21 goals, McLaughlin and Sinclair 20, Melrose on 16, Smith 10.

It is all the more remarkable then that early in 1965–66, Sinclair, Melrose, McLaughlin and Kilgannon all left the club. Not surprisingly Bert really made the breakthrough. Willie Cunningham could hardly have failed to notice him, what with his goal scoring romps with the reserves topped off with scoring a double hat-trick in one. After a shock home defeat by Dundee United, Cunningham brought him back into the first team. For much of the season the Pars regular team would be:- Martin, Callaghan, Lunn, Smith, McLean, T Callaghan, Edwards, Paton, Fleming, Ferguson, Robertson. On 6th November the pencil slim inside right put three past St Mirren in a 5–1 home win. He would go on to score 25 in an incredible season when the first team would amass 131, Fergie accounting for 39 of them. 'Fergie was great to play beside. He was a poacher par excellence always finishing a ball that came back off the bar or goalie. I think I only once saw him score from more than 18 yards'! Two of his 5 European goals came against the Danish Bold Klub in Round 2 of the Fairs Cup. In the league, dominated that year by the Old Firm, Paton was scoring consistently but one goal really stood out. On Boxing Day the Pars were at Ibrox and coming off a 0–2 home defeat by Celtic. Despite losing a goal in the opening minute, they took the game to Rangers with a pace and zest the Glasgow team could not match. Hughie Robertson scored two but Bert's 30 yard screamer to Ritchie's left was the one to savour. The crowd met it all in their traditional Ibrox silence. Bert was revelling in the 4–4–2 system which entailed Fleming and Ferguson playing up front and splitting the defence to allow Paton to play effectively just behind them. In Europe the Pars put out Spartak Brno in Round 3 and met Real Zaragoza in the

Quarter-Final. A ropey Pars performance and an ultra-defensive Spanish team combined to fend off the Athletic till Paton scored 3 minutes from the end from an Edwards inch perfect cross.

A lot of the fans were already heading to the exits. 'I'll never forget the stick I took from the players after that goal. I was having a nightmare match, in fact so much so the players said, get out to the wing! Well in the dying minutes I moved into the centre, scored that goal and the following morning the sports pages were describing me as the Pars saviour'! They eventually went down 4–3 on aggregate. Bert was beginning to pick up a few pointers from Willie Cunningham. 'As in the Stein era every player was made to feel he'd something to offer, the team was more important than the individual. A lot of the players were local and that encouraged both loyalty and team spirit. Cunningham made some inspired signings. There was no place for a Prima Donna, the club paid well and the manager was hard but fair.' As league form tailed off, attention turned to the Cup again. Paton scored 3 goals in the wins over Partick Thistle and Stirling, setting up a cracker against provincial rivals Killie. 20,000 witnessed a sensational game that cold March day in which Paton equalised and Alex Edwards scored his last gasp winner. They went down to Celtic in the Cup Semi-Final. By Dunfermline's own high standards, 1966–67 was to prove a relatively disappointing season with the club slipping from fourth to eighth position and Bert scoring 10 goals. 'But that season there were two of the most memorable games I ever played in' says Bert without hesitation. 'There's no denying that my most important games were the 1968 Scottish Cup Final and the European Cup Winners Cup Semi-Final in 1969 but I will never forget the 5–6 defeat by Hibs in the September and the 4–5 defeat by Celtic that November in which I scored.' In choosing these two matches, Bert outlines his whole philosophy towards the game. As his team formations and tactics 1993–1996 displayed, what mattered was that Paton's teams attacked, entertained and scored goals. That was certainly true of both these games. In the former Hibs, 0–3 up at half time raced to a 0–4 lead after one hour, then the fight back began. The Athletic pulled back to 2–4. In the 84th minute the Fifers had it back to 5–5 before Scott scored against the Pars reserve keeper. It 'rained goals' again in the Celtic match. 'It was also daylight robbery' says Bert. 'The match went off like a rocket with the Pars 3–2 up at half-time. I scored the third, nipping in to poach one as 2 Celtic defenders left it to each other. With the score at 4–4 it went into the last minute and the 20,000 crowd was at fever pitch as the play swung from end to end. Suddenly Chalmers seemed to head past the post a McBride knock on from an Auld free kick with Roy Barry marking him. As the ref dashed up field, the linesman's flag went up. He'd seen something and McBride, a player Cunningham had one tried to sign, scored the resultant penalty. It was desperate we'd put so much into it to gain no reward.'

In September 1966 the Athletic signed a cult figure. Roy Barry moved from Hearts, after months of negotiations and he played as the Pars put Frigg out of the Fairs Cup on a 6–2 aggregate. Paton, as usual, enjoyed the trip to Norway. 'Then we lost to Dinamo Zagreb 4–4 on aggregate having won at East End 4–2 because the new away goals rule had just come in' Bert explains. Dunfermline beat Rangers home and away but the league season was disappointing, and there was no prospect of qualifying for Europe. In the Cup, victories over Kilmarnock and Partick Thistle were followed by defeat 1–0 at Tannadice, but Paton's finest hour, as a player, was about to dawn. As the new season began there would be no European distractions but a new manager in place. For some time Cunningham had expressed himself sick to death of the whole business of football management and the Board allowed the disillusioned manager to break free of his contract. He said he'd no intention of taking on the role again. In October he became manager of Falkirk. Nearly every big name applied for the post but it went to George Farm at Raith Rovers, a man with Scottish Caps and an FA Cup winners medal. He had just taken Raith up to Division 1. With Fergie going to Rangers for a then record fee of £60,000, Farm snapped up Pat Gardner and Ian Lister from the Kirkcaldy club. They would win the Pars the Scottish Cup. 'I'd enjoyed a good relationship on the pitch with Fergie and this was to continue with Pat. Pat was a very different player from Fergie, he was more of a footballer and the fans never fully appreciated his contribution. He shielded the ball, had a great shot and scored and made goals' recalls Bert. 'Bert's unselfish style of play encouraged both to the best football of their careers' was Duncan Simpson's assessment. With Farm 'a hard man' in Paton's view, in charge, Dunfermline were in 6th position come Christmas. Losing the first 3 home league matches did not help nor did it in anyway suggest the glory yet to come. On New Year's Day though Dunfermline destroyed Raith 6–0 in the derby match with Paton scoring 3.

In the view of this writer, we witnessed one of the Pars greatest goals, when Paton took a ball from Callaghan and seemingly tackled the entire Raith team before coolly walking the ball into the net! 'My favourite ground was always Tynecastle and the next day we won a league match there for the first time so clearly things were improving'. They had to. The Pars were now drawn to meet the European Cup holders and the League Champions Celtic at Parkhead in the Cup. In an 18 goal season, Paton would only score 2 in the Cup but they could hardly have been more important. 'I have 2 abiding memories of that wonderful game. On the way to Parkhead, we found ourselves having lunch in the same Glasgow hotel as Hibs, who were on their way to Hamilton. The players got chatting and the Edinburgh lads were stunned to learn the bonus we were on. I learned later they almost went on strike! The match itself was a remarkable achievement and we were all fired up after poor Jim Fraser got stretchered off.' After the sensational 0–2 win at Parkhead, Dunfermline defeated Aberdeen 2–1, the winner scored 5 minutes from time by Edwards after it was held up by Bert. In the Quarter-Final, in a match of missed chances, it seemed George Niven would keep the Athletic at bay till a single goal by Paton in the 80th minute settled it. The Athletic were overwhelming favourites for the Semi-Final in late March at Tynecastle but Bert, who'd scored a hat-trick against Morton days earlier, was to be involved in a fluke equaliser which spared the Fife club's blushes. The relegation threatened Perth team took the lead in the 4th minute and the Pars only equalised in the 53rd when Paton blocked a clearance by Saints goalie Robertson. The ball cannoned off his body to Gardner who slotted it into the empty net. The Saints scored first again in the replay but Paton equalised from a Gardner cross. Robertson missed a penalty and Paton the resultant rebound, before a great goal by Lister sealed it.

On 27th April, 56,365 saw Paton play the most important match of his life when Dunfermline beat Hearts 3–1 in the Cup Final. 'Although denied a lap of honour at Hampden, I will never forget the rapturous welcome of the 25,000 crowd in the High Street as the open topped bus took us down to meet their acclaim on the balcony at the city Chambers as they played Cliff Richard's 'Congratulations' at full volume. If we won the Cup today there would be a party, high jinks and celebrations all through the night but remarkably, in those days, you'd a celebratory toast and then we all said 'goodnight' and went our separate ways into the night. I ended up having a fish supper in Halbeath on my way home.' 27,816 and more saw the Cup holders and League Champions meet at East End three days later, to bring down the curtain on a fabulous season. Celtic won 1–2, not that it mattered, and in devilment big Jock tried to prise the Cup away from Farm's hands! 1968–69 began in rather erratic fashion in terms of league results yet the club would finish 3rd in the table equalling their best.

However the season is best remembered for the exploits in the European Cup Winners Cup. Dunfermline romped home 12–1 on aggregate against Apoel Nicosia to give the players a nice break in Cyprus, remarkably Bert didn't score. The second Round was totally different. They needed every goal of the 4–0 first leg at home to survive (and that was the operative word) against Olympiakos of Greece on a 4–3 aggregate. 'I didn't even get to the second leg. As we scored one of our goals I was simply knocked out and I was left staggering around the park. I spent that night in hospital. That set up a cracker of a Quarter-Final against England's representatives West Brom including their star striker Jeff Astle. East End was at a capacity 25,000 for the first leg but, despite some devastating football, we just could not put the ball in the net. 2000 Pars fans travelled to the Hawthorns, over 10,000 were at East End in a gale watching on giant screens, a real novelty in 1969. I'll never forget Pat Gardner's goal. Alex Edwards took a free kick on the bone hard pitch, it came back

Dunfermline players celebrate the triumph over West Brom in 1969.

off a defender. This time he got it to Pat who headed it home. It's not often a Scottish club has put out one in England but Roy Barry led us for 88 minutes in a superb rear guard action. I still feel the bitterly cold frosty conditions helped us too.' In the Semi-Final the Athletic were paired with the Czechoslovakian Cup holders Slovan Bratislava and only 16,559 supporters watched the first leg at East End 'Yet it was probably the most important match Dunfermline ever played' says Bert. When Chairman Andrew Watson said in the programme that we should remind ourselves how far Dunfermline had now come because so rarely did the club gain the recognition deserved for all their achievements, it was a sentiment often echoed in 1996. After relentless pressure Jim Fraser, the defender so cruelly left out of the 1968 Cup Final side, scored just on half time as Paton cut back an Edwards free from the right touchline. 'When the Czechoslovakians equalised our task was enormous.' Slovan who went on to win the Cup won the second leg 1–0. Gardner and Paton were the season's main goal scorers with 17 and 16 goals respectively. In October they were actually top of the league and were to beat Aberdeen on one occasion 5–1 but 3–0 and 3–1 defeats at Ibrox and Parkhead took their toll. It was in the Cup that the Dons took their revenge. The Athletic had been confident of retaining the trophy and dispatched Raith (away) 0–2 with Paton scoring. However, the Dons won at East End 0–2 after drawing 2–2 at Pittodrie. As the season ended John Hunter discovered that the Board met to discuss how much of a bonus they'd give the manager were he to win a European Trophy! As for Bert, he offered to play for the second team. His goals were unaccountably drying up and he hadn't scored since a game at Arbroath in mid-February. Paton's golden age as an Athletic player was nearing its end. However, the start of 1969–70 didn't suggest this.

One new player at the club was George McLean, the former Ranger for whom the Pars paid a record fee. Even he couldn't alter the club's annual abysmal form in the League Cup. Through the autumn the Athletic were consistently among the top 2 in the league and against this backdrop they met Bordeaux in the Fairs Cup. Bert Paton was mightily relieved to score two smartly taken goals in a 4–0 win then the team survived a brutal mauling in France to take the tie 4–2 on aggregate. 'Bordeaux was undoubtedly my worst experience in Europe. The home crowd was seething and our players agreed to meet in the centre circle at the end and head to the dressing room together but we were kicked in the ribs as we ran back and the crowd then hammered on our door to get in. We'd to get a police escort out of the ground. I played with a poisoned leg after an injury I sustained in that first leg.' Bert was out till mid-November when he scored in the 4–2 home win over Airdrie. His only other league goal came one month later in the home defeat 2–3 by Dundee United. Significantly, by then, Roy Barry was gone and they slumped to an unaccustomed mid-table position. Some entertainment was provided by winger Jim Gillespie signed from Raith, one of the cult figures in the club's history. In the Fairs Cup they went on to defeat Gwardia Warsaw 3–1 (aggregate) but few realised when they beat Anderlecht 3–2 (3–3 aggregate) on the 14th of January 1970, that 11,773 had witnessed the club's last appearance in Europe. It just seemed unthinkable. Bert was not involved. In the

79th minute of the match against Dundee United on 10th December, in which he scored in the defeat he broke his right leg; the whole ground hearing the horrible click. He was out for the rest of the season. In those days there was a brand new medical plastic bag, which the club had acquired, to wrap around a broken leg immediately. However, there had been bad condensation and the seams got frayed. As I came off It gave no support at all. As I lay in the dressing room Roy Barry told me forward Alan Gordon had done it, a more unlikely player was impossible to imagine.' The following year the season began disastrously and in October 1970 George Farm was sacked. Alex Wright became manager and the club narrowly avoided relegation. The Cup squad broke up and, with the emphasis now on youth and no money to spend, it was urgent that Paton returned to the team after 18 long months out. 'I was working hard to get back in the team and even joined some professional sprinters to get my sharpness back. Then, that November at Hibs, I broke the same leg again.' In April 1972 Paton decided to call it a day. He had scored 86 goals, 7 in Europe. He was 27.

After leaving the club he was a car salesman, a grocer and a very popular publican in Rosyth. After a spell as manager at Cowdenbeath and Raith, and then coach at Hearts, assistant manager at Dumbarton (a really happy period) he moved to St Johnstone. In his first year as assistant to Alex Totten they took the Perth team to Division 1 then, with the new stadium at McDiarmid Park, they won the Championship in 1990. Inexplicably he was sacked in 1992. Totten followed soon afterwards, and the Saints returned to Division 1 in an episode similar to the Leishman affair. He then worked for 'CR Smith' beside Dick Campbell and the pair teamed up at Rosyth Recreation FC. In 1993, Jocky Scott was sacked and, after a wait of 21 years, Bert got the call he'd always dreamed of. Dunfermline had been relegated in 1992 with an abysmal 18 points from 44 games. In 1992–93 the season had begun with promise and ended with disappointment, the club throwing away a 7 point lead over Kilmarnock. Dunfermline fans were sickened by the defensive tactics, culminating in a humiliating 0–2 home defeat by already relegated Cowdenbeath, a game in which the Pars played with one up front. Noisy scenes by fans outside the ground against Jocky Scott, after the final home defeat by Morton, ensured Scott's demise. 'I didn't even tell Dick at "CR Smith" that I was being interviewed, along with the likes of Alex Totten and Murdo MacLeod. When I got the job, I got out my old Pars no. 8 strip, put it on the peg and sat under it for the photographers. I had to bring back the good old days and my strip was a link with the past.' As Paton took over as manager, he was well aware of the lack of morale, the gloom and despondency which had descended on the club since Jim Leishman left. 'It was a morgue' he says pointedly 'I had to get the players believing in themselves again and enjoying their football.' After a close season of turmoil the fans took immediately to the new management team of Campbell and Paton.

At the first match on 31 July 1993, Dunfermline set out their stall, showing in the 2–1 friendly win over West Ham, in which cult figure Ivo Den Bieman made his debut, that they would play attacking football. In his first ever 'Paton's Pars' column he wrote 'I can promise you 2 things. First we will not fail through lack of effort. Second, only people who want to play for Dunfermline Athletic will be out there on the park.' The fans knew they had a fellow Fifer in charge, a former player, and someone who lived for the club. They stayed with him when the Pars played flowing attractive attacking football but lost the opening three league games. 'I remember, after those early defeats, Hugh Keevins of *The Scotsman* was very critical and phoned the chairman to ask how happy was he now with his new management team? Well, a few days later, he came through to broadcast on our midweek game with Rangers. Dick and I sought him out, up in the stand, and chose some pretty strong language to express our disquiet. Then, to our horror, we realised he was wearing a microphone and the whole of Scotland had heard our torrent of abuse, live!' Paton was mightily relieved when they finally beat Airdrie 3–2, though he was not going to change tactics. George O'Boyle ended up top goalscorer with 19 of the league goals, as the club was pipped by 1 point by Falkirk, a 1–1 home draw before 13,357 fans with the eventual champions in March, proving costly. However, it was the astonishing 1–0 defeat on 7th May in

Airdrie's last match at Broomfield that effectively ended the challenge, yet the Pars played the Diamonds off the park. 'We really were put off by all the emotional pre-match build up, it being the final game at Broomfield. We sat for ages in the dressing room waiting for those parachutists to arrive with the ball and it affected our nerves.' 6,163 cheered the Pars hoarse in the final home game as the Pars players, many of them in tears, were forced to take a lap of honour. The seasons final overall attendance was 115,000. Slowly but surely the team he wanted was taking shape as Paton added Petrie from Forfar, Tod from Kelty and Moore from St Johnstone to the first team. He had all the skill of a George Miller in wheeling and dealing in the transfer market. 'I'd to keep the club's bankers as happy as the fans' he recalls wryly. At the start of 1994–95, Bert Paton told the fans he welcomed the introduction of 3 points for a win because too many teams in the division' only aspired to retaining the point they began the match with.' (Had the scheme operated one season earlier, Dunfermline would have been the Champions.) As the season began, Chairman Roy Woodrow paid tribute to the attractive brand of football Paton and Campbell were encouraging against the back drop of the club being in financial difficulties.

Such problems meant that few improvements could be made to the stadium. However, it was not only income from the gate which was being generated, on the commercial front some of the club's best ever results were being achieved thanks largely to the tireless efforts of manageress Audrey Bastianelli. That was a good thing because, having made a good start to the campaign including an excellent 1–0 home win over Raith Rovers, Bert Paton was looking forward to having the rare opportunity to spend some real money at last. Class act Irishman George O'Boyle, the club's top goalscorer with 19 goals the previous season, had moved to St Johnstone under freedom of contract in the close season, a move which did not endear him to the Pars fans, after the time, money and assistance the club gave him as he recovered from cruciate ligament damage. No player, in the 1990s, has been booed to the rafters to quite such the same extent on his subsequent appearances. Having scored a hat-trick the previous week, and being included in the Northern Ireland squad, the club's case at the tribunal seemed cast iron. Lord McCluskey and his committee, in their wisdom, granted a miserly £200,000 yet he'd already scored 8 goals for the Perth team. Duncan Simpson in the 'Pars Programme' later asked how Dunfermline could possibly replace a player of that calibre with such a sum? They took special pleasure in defeating St Johnstone convincingly 3–0 that October! On a happier note, Norrie McCathie made his 500th official appearance in league and Cup games in a Coca-Cola game against Meadowbank scoring his 50th goal in the process. Bert, though, made it plain that autumn that they needed a larger pool. The division was now even tougher than the previous one, as three teams had just come down from the Premier and 5 had dropped to Division '2. First he moved for outstanding Meadowbank left-full back Derek Fleming, who made such a memorable debut against St Johnstone. The same October Paton snapped up versatile Brechin midfielder Marc Millar for £60,000, a player he said later he'd tracked for a year. He added quality to a team which, unbelievably, ripped promotion favourites Raith apart away 2–5 and then followed that up with a 4–1 win over Clydebank making the subsequent 3–1 defeat at Hamilton all the more incomprehensible. As 1994 ended, Bert was becoming increasingly concerned at the number of away draws. No longer was 1 away point as in a 0–0 draw at Stranraer, of much value. These results were later to haunt the club. Even worse was a 3–2 defeat at Boxing Day in Perth when the Fifers had been 0–2 up. By the time 9416 watched the postponed New Year defeat by Raith 0–1 Bert says 'I was now enquiring after Maurice Johnston and Frank McAvennie. We were not scoring many goals and what we did get was coming from midfield.' Even so as the Pars moved into the last quarter they were still top of the league and 2 points clear of Dundee and Raith.

The one player they had signed was former United goalie Guido van de Kamp. Then things went very wrong. 'We really needed everyone for the run in but we lost Kenny Ward for the remainder of the season and, indeed, the one that followed, then there was the awful injury to Hamish French which put him out as well, in addition to the usual injuries and suspensions.' Bert Paton said on 1st April that 'he was glad to say he'd entered the transfer market and signed Falkirk's Greg Shaw.' In fact he'd desperately wanted the Board to sanction a £100,000 bid for 19 goal Peter Duffield with mid-table Hamilton and they'd only allowed £20,000 for Shaw, a player coming back from injury and languishing in the reserves at Brockville. In his eight sub-sequent appearances Shaw did not score once! Dunfermline took 17 points from the quarter frustratingly drawing 5 of them. Dunfermline always had it in their own hands to gain promotion but a home draw 0–0 with Airdrie and a similar away result at Starks Park, where the Raith tactics were similar to those the Americans used at the Alamo, ended another frustrating season.

The club was now into the new play offs. Incredibly Dunferm-line found themselves up against one of the biggest teams in the land, Aberdeen, a team, ironically, bang on form. The Pars put up a gallant effort up at Pittodrie going down 3–1 before 19,387 but, having a stone wall penalty turned down probably affected them psychologically. 15,977 attended the second leg at East End despite live TV coverage, but the extra man, the huge support entailed, could not shout their heroes to victory and the score was repeated. Duncan Shearer of Aberdeen said later 'It's a crime for a club like that to be in division 1'! Joe Harper, the former Dons hero, added 'There's no question but McKimmie tripped Dun-fermline's Alan Moore.' In years to come, I dare say there'll be one other aspect of that second leg the fans will readily recall. Astonished, taken aback, or even outraged by the unprecedented tannoy build up at Pittodrie, the Pars tannoy announcer Alex Mill used a lot of his own psychology at East End with a build up to the game never before heard or equalled! His 'over the top' lingering over each of the Pars players and their achievements, the wonderful playing of 'Nessun Dorma' full blast, the racing through the Aberdeen team sheet and the exhortation to the crowd to get behind the team, all were just superb. The Pars had got some revenge at last. Bert reflects 'I am often asked how he coped with the disappointment in the summers of 1994 and 1995. We coped really well. In fact we all went off to the Med and had a great time. There was no difficulty at all getting the players spirits up for the new campaign. Football is fun. These should, surely, be the best years of the players lives; they should come off the park smiling. If they don't, I pull them into my office and get them to put on my old C.R. Smith overalls. Then I say, would you rather do an 8-hour factory shift, with just 20 minutes for a tea break?' As 1995–96 began, the media took it for granted that Dundee United whom Bert Paton described as 'Rangers reserves', would run away with the Title. Their European pedigree, stadium, size of squad, the support, Premier set up, internationalists and cheque book seemed to make it all a foregone conclusion. Dunfermline had long term injuries to Ward and French and Andy Smith - Andy having contrived to break a leg just after his signing from Airdrie in a pre-season friendly! In any case even if the Pars did well, they'd 'bottle it' all in the run in, said the West of Scotland media, assuredly. Shaw scored at last in the opening game at Airdrie and then the Pars did their 'talking on the park' as they destroyed Dundee United 3–0 at home at the end of August. The Athletic took an impressive 21 points in the first quarter yet lost to Dundee 0–1 (with Paul Smith latterly playing in goal) and Morton 0–2 the other 2 main rivals.

In October, Paton lost Jackie McNamara to Celtic for £600,000, a record for the club. 'Nobody wanted to see him go, particularly me, but I had to get the club on a sound financial footing' Paton says 'and the bank would not allow us to wait till we were in the Premier Division to sell him and probably get more.' Later that month, as the injury hit Pars lost 3–1 at United, the West of Scotland tabloids agreed that the Dundee United team would win the flag, the Athletic had been so outclassed. As the Athletic had remained on top of the league from day one, the media obstinately gave the club little credit or space, especially the *Daily Record*, for their achievement. At the half-way stage, the club was better off for points than in 1994 with the most noticeable improvement being in away results with six wins compared to only two. 'Looking back on that improvement, you have to remember that French, Robertson, Cooper, Millar etc all have coaching certificates and their experience had a great affect on the younger lads.' As the year ended they lost again to Morton 0–2 at home, to St Johnstone 1–0 away but beat Dundee 2–4 at Dens. Canadian full back Colin Miller came from Hearts in the Paul Smith exchange. Hamish French was back from injury. By

January Bert Paton had to cope with the tragic death of Norrie McCathie and the feeling was that either the team, newly knocked off their top of the table perch, would now collapse or they would carry on with a grim new determination and clinch the Championship which meant so much to them. Paton was utterly determined it would be the latter. In February 8400 saw Dunfermline and Dundee United fight out a 2–2 home draw just a week after Dundee United put Dunfermline out of the Cup 1–0 at Tannadice. The Athletic were gaining considerably from the reappearance of former Airdrie star, Andy Smith, who was now fully recovered from the leg break. The Athletic now embarked on a sensational run which would include a 3–2 win over St Johnstone, in which new signing from Falkirk, John Clark, scored one of the greatest Pars goals ever, and a 4–1 thrashing of Morton both at home, and gaining a fortuitous 2–2 draw away to St Johnstone. Nothing though surely, could equal the fantastic 0–1 Dunfermline win at Tannadice on 27th April, 22 years to the day since they'd last won there. On Bert's desk a sign reads 'The greatest crime in football is to give the ball to the opposition.' 'I felt at the time that this game would be the Championship decider and so it proved. Anyone who doubts our support is a 12th man should have heard the volume they made that day.'

The Pars certainly remembered that motto in this game. After one week of Pars fans replaying their video of Stewart Petrie's goal over and over again, Dunfermline took on Airdrie in the full knowledge that a win would mean the flag regardless of the score at Cappielow. When Bert got the Dunfermline post he said 'If I went tomorrow I would die happy having got the job I always wanted.' Now, having given the fans what they wanted most, you suspect that, from here on in, everything else will be just a bonus. Paton does not agree 'I would still like to re-establish Dunfermline in the top five in Scotland and see us back in Europe. If I once achieve that I would gladly hand over the reins to a younger man.' In a season in which Paton complained about the lack of recognition the Athletic received for their achievement, he was the only manager not to receive the Divisional manager of the year award at the seasons end, for winning the league; the division 1 award going to Morton's McGraw. *Plus ça change...*

51

—4—

NORRIE McCATHIE 1961–1996

Every fan of Dunfermline Athletic knows where they were and what they were doing on Monday evening, 8th January, when they learned, with total incredulity, that Norrie was dead. A handful learned at the reserve match with St Johnstone, where Bert Paton was given the heartbreaking news by police officers. His two pubs, D'Arcy's and East Port, which he owned with John Watson, were unaccountably closed, as was his night club, Nico's.

Rumours of the tragedy thus swept the town all evening but, by the morning, the media confirmed that the young footballer found dead in his cottage, just outside the town, was indeed Norrie. The older generation talked of not knowing such an outpouring of communal grief locally since the death of President John F Kennedy in 1963. TV had made the world a global village and people felt they knew the President. Some only knew Norrie from TV too, but many thousands had been entertained by him on the park, and a considerable number knew him at first hand, because Norrie was not only a star performer on the pitch; he was a magnificent ambassador for the club, an astute local businessman and a very human person with his own private life. Some friends remarked that Norrie seemed to be good at everything he put his hand to. He did a huge amount of charity work, a lot of it on the quiet, and he would invariably visit children in hospital at a moment's notice. He was committed to the Dunfermline Half Marathon and, with his partner John Watson, he presented a trophy in memory of Gary Riddell, the other Athletic player who'd died tragically in June 1989. He switched on the town's Christmas lights, led the torchlight procession on occasion, took part in the charity 'It's a Knockout', raised money for hospitals and voluntary groups and coached kids at football. He always took time out to sign autographs, notably at the Centenary club's sponsored Christmas Panto evening at the Carnegie Hall and he had time for everyone and seemed to be the friend of all. Norrie's final match had been the innocuous 2–1 defeat at Love Street, the first in about a month and maybe it was appropriate that the Pars were, temporarily, knocked off their perch at the top of the table. In a very quiet, stunned dressing room new captain Craig Robertson spoke for all the players when he said 'The players are united in wanting to go on and win the title for Norrie. As the gaffer said, that would be the greatest tribute we could ever pay him.' Meanwhile, Norrie's family gave the go-ahead to the match against Clydebank going ahead. This was an irony, as Clydebank, of all teams in Scotland, knew precisely what the Fife club was going through. Clydebank Director Ian Steedman, looking back on the tragic premature death of Davie Cooper said 'I know what it will be like at Dunfermline; playing football will be the last thing on their minds.

There are times when the game becomes trivial, the players will be shattered and it will take a very, very long time to get over the death of such a stalwart.' If anyone not associated with the club was in any doubt about how devastated the district was, the appearance of scarves, pennants, wreaths, flowers, teddy bears, rosettes and tammies — the length of the pavement outside the stadium, about half way out to the road, as the week wore on, dispelled that doubt. The thousands of scarves would later end up in Romania and Bosnia. Some were from Fife clubs, local rivals Falkirk, league contenders Dundee United, the large city clubs and the littlest, as Scotland displayed yet again, we are a nation of communities and they too shared our sadness. Thousands looked up at least one evening that week and stood heads bowed in the rain, silent in their memories. Meanwhile, tributes were flooding in from the supporters, the licensed trade community, politicians, local businesses, charities, other football clubs and the players. Craig Robertson called him 'a great leader who led by example', Stewart Petrie 'he was the unofficial ambassador for the town', Allan Moore called him 'a friendly man who didn't have a bad word for anyone.' Kenny Ward recalled 'there was never a bad word even if you played against him', Neale Cooper described him as 'a truly great professional and a delight to play alongside', Jackie McNamara of Celtic 'he was so easy going and had a huge influence on me', Ian Westwater made the significant point 'Jim Leishman and Gregor Abel shaped so much at this club but Norrie played a huge part too', Guido van de Kamp said 'Norrie was irreplaceable', Paul Smith (Hearts) explained 'the fans loved him because he always led from the front',

Hamish French highlighted 'Norrie's positive attitude which rubbed off on all of us'. Andy Tod called him 'a smashing bloke', Ivo den Bieman stressed ' how ambitious he always was for the club and you never saw him under pressure', Grant Jenkins recalled 'he was the life and soul of the club when I was there and Andy Rhodes (Airdrie) mentioned 'a loyalty you so rarely see given to any club today. I hope the Athletic go on now to win the championship.' Former manager Jim Leishman said 'I could only do so much to motivate the team in the dressing room, Norrie did the rest on the field'; Jocky Scott called him 'a natural leader', Iain Munro added 'he was Mr Reliable — he always gave 100%', Pat Stanton remembered 'a tremendous leader' and Gordon Wallace said, poignantly, 'you can't imagine Dunfermline without him'. Jimmy Nicholl added 'his death was a huge loss to football in general.' In the award winning 'Pars Programme' Duncan Simpson wrote 'As well as widespread respect, opponents came to fear him — feared because of his commitment and passion for the Pars, for his fight and drive that could turn around a seemingly hopeless position. Despite his enormous will to win, his endless battling qualities, there wasn't an ounce of malice in his entire body. He was an absolute gentleman — that is why so many players and supporters of other clubs have left messages of sympathy and mementos at East End Park and have shared in our grief. Norrie proved an inspiration to hundreds of players, some who made it, some who didn't — who passed through the gates of the club over the years.'

Meanwhile, as the Clydebank match approached, training resumed and Bert Paton, who'd broken down at the Press Conference, called to discuss the tragedy, knew he had to get the players' heads up so he held a team meeting at which they all discussed the good times and their favourite memories. It was to hit home to the supporters that Norrie really was gone when the team ran out, led by Craig Robertson, on Saturday afternoon 13th on a cold grey, grim Fife day in keeping with the numbness of people's feelings. Graham Speirs in *Scotland on Sunday* commented 'you couldn't help picturing a face.' In praise of the players' tributes to the man, which so often recalled the fact he was anything but a snappy dresser, Spiers said 'these were not inappropriate remarks, they had the authenticating seal of real, true friendship.' One of the most moving tributes was to come from manager Paton with a feel for the right idiom. 'Norrie was not just Paton's Par' he wrote 'He was, to everybody who knew and loved him, the Par of this or any other decade. When I think about all the great Dunfermline players of the past, Norrie is up there with the very best of them. His immense loyalty to the Pars and also to the local community earned him the title 'Mr Dunfermline'. On the park I could not have asked for better. He was remarkable and consistent, a strong leader and a really genuine guy. He was also a truly inspirational captain. Norrie's famous saying before games was 'If you don't want to wear the jersey, stay in the dressing room.' Chairman Roy Woodrow took the opportunity to say 'that those who comment that Dunfermline players do not really want promotion should have seen Norrie in tears at the end of the previous season.' Dick Campbell wrote 'His memory and inspiration will live at this club for a very long time.' 6,642 turned up for the match in his honour and how Norrie would have revelled in a game in which Dunfermline raced to a 3–0 lead, then witnessed Clydebank, who earlier had taken part in the 2 minutes silence and then ran across to the home terracings to emotionally applaud the Pars support, pull back all 3 goals, only for a colossal drive by new captain Craig Robertson to win the day. Thousands of fans raced onto the pitch and adorned the home goal nets with more of their scarves at the end. The following Tuesday morning 6000 fans, and managers, coaches and players from every league club in Scotland attended the memorial service at East End. Dunfermline Athletic rested the no. 4 jersey for the remainder of the season. 'No one else was big enough to wear it' said Bert Paton.

Let's move back to happier times. In the autumn of 1995 I interviewed Norrie for his chapter in this book. I had first met him in 1987 and interviewed him on a number of occasions mainly for *Scottish Football Today* magazine. His place in any history of Dunfermline Athletic was, as Paton said in his tribute, always guaranteed. His tragic death robbed the team captain of a place in Scottish football history though, in the sense that only a dozen players made Scottish 500 league appearances for one club, yet he was only days away from achieving that at East End. In total he made 561 appearances for the Athletic and scored 59 goals - not bad going for a defender! His 497 league appearances put Bobby Robertson on 360 in 2nd place and Kenny Thomson on 354 in 3rd. He was the 8th highest league scorer for the Pars in the post-war period and came 13th in the Scottish league appearance for one club 'roll of honour.'

'I first kicked a ball in the shadow of Easter Road, would you believe?' he told me. 'I was a striker with Edinburgh amateur side Edina Hibs and I scored 38 goals.' 'Cowdenbeath manager Pat Stanton was tipped off about me and I signed for the princely sum of £350, but I never got my small cut! I played a handful of games for them but didn't get a goal. Although I come from Leith, I was a Hearts fan and yes, I was at the 7–0 defeat by Hibs which is not one of my happiest memories. Pat Stanton moved to East End and I wasn't getting a game under Andy Rolland so I was delighted when a player exchange was arranged with Craig MacFarlane. At that time all this meant to me was more money. A lot of players came to the club at the time, the biggest name being the Dons' Considine for £43000, but there were also Hugh Hamill, Jim Brown and George Young. After 2 months I got my first game in the October at Ayr deputising for Kevin Hegarty. I made 17 appearances, and scored 4 times from midfield, the first being against Queen's Park.' Programme editor Duncan Simpson discovered that on McCathie's first appearance in a back 4, the Pars conceded 6 goals to Motherwell! The 6 foot 12 stone defender had no doubts about his role at the club. 'For the first 4 years at Dunfermline I was being used as a utility player. I wouldn't claim the credit for the positional change either. In February 1985 Jim Leishman tried an experiment in a match against the league leaders Alloa at Recreation Park. We got a shock 3–1 win that day and I played sweeper for the first time wearing the no. 4 jersey.' In his first season at East End, the Dunfermline Board may have speculated about promotion, in reality they flirted with relegation and went down at the end of 1982–3. One year later, under Jim Leishman, they were an abysmal 9th in Division 2 but things were improving in 1985 when they were pipped for promotion by one point. Against that

Norrie — an inspirational captain

back drop, Norrie's appearances and goals were both on the increase. He scored 10 goals in 1984–5 and played in all 44 league games in 1986–87. The player, who still worked as a whisky blender in Leith, and who described his Dad as 'the biggest influence on my career', was now forming a lethal strike force with Grant Jenkins and pal John Watson. Jim Leishman says 'Norrie had great strength in the opposition box but I felt his contribution over the 90 minutes was not sufficient and his passing could have been more accurate.

We were losing too many silly goals at the time so I moved him to shake up the defence! Players who played beside him like Grant Tierney, Davie Young and Grant Reid told me, later, they had played the best football of their careers beside him. He was one of the strongest players and best tacklers Dunfermline ever had and perhaps the most underestimated. He always fought to the last minute as his equaliser in a 3–3 game at Forfar and last gasp winner in a 0–1 thriller at Clyde proved. On that second occasion he won the ball in his own box, interpassed to the half way line, took on the whole Clyde defence and stabbed it home. I used to keep telling him I made him one of the best centre backs ever! To be serious though, no one deserved a testimonial more than Norrie. He wasn't just a player, he became a fan and, though many talent scouts watched him, there was no way he would ever go.' In 1985–6 he was a major factor in the club's championship success story. He had become one of the most commanding defenders for the club in many years. He had superb ability in the air in either attack or defence, had great vision with his passing, his timing was immaculate and he read the game well. When the team won promotion to the Premier in 1987 he was selected by Craig Brown for the Scotland semi-professional team. You would imagine that he would single out the 1st Division Championship in 1989 or the Skol Cup Final 1991 appearance as his most cherished memories but no. 'There was no feeling to compare with the emotion of winning the 2nd Division Championship medal back in 1986' he pointed out emphatically. On the occasions I spoke to him, I always felt that it was not just his obvious skills on the field of play which had been so crucial, the bronzed moustachioed figure exuded the sort of confidence and determination for which Souness was renowned. He was also a real character off the park - stories of his dressing room pranks were legion. As Dunfermline bounded from Division 2 to Division 1 to the Premier, his critics always came out with the comment that this season would be the last. He was getting slower, he would not be able to cope etc.

When the club reached the Premier and full-time football returned many of the Pars players, who had taken them there, moved on but Norrie simply adapted to the higher level and confounded the critics. Players were brought in to replace him but they all failed. However, he did not find it easy. 'We took some hammerings in our first season at the top level. Part of the reason was that a lot of new players came in, but we were also up against class players who were a yard or two quicker. They seemed to think and react more quickly and you couldn't even make one mistake. It took some time to adjust. One thing that helped was our crowd. With 6000 or more the atmosphere generated was great.' In 1988–89 he made a bad start to the Division 1 Championship winning season when a bad injury in a preseason match put him out for almost three months and he even had a loan spell at Ayr to get fit. With Riddell and Tierney playing well he did not gain a regular place again till early 1989.

He had only featured in 19 league games when he held the trophy aloft now as the permanent captain that May. One of Jim Leishman's fondest memories of Norrie was of him swinging from the rafters at the after match celebrations. 'The team of 1989–90 including Kozma, O'Boyle, McCall, and Watson ('the best player in Scotland') was the best Dunfermline had in my time', Norrie argues.

Norrie would never comment on the events of summer 1990. Indeed Duncan Simpson argues this was always a major McCathie strength. He would never criticise anyone himself, not a ref or opponent or colleague or manager. All Norrie would say about morale at the club was 'There was a good positive reaction to the management changes when Bert and Dick came.' Later that summer, Norrie had his testimonial match and 6000 attended including recently deposed Jim Leishman who did not have to come disguised! A host of former stars including Alex Smith, Jackie Sinclair, Alex Edwards, Willie Callaghan, Jim Thomson, Harry Melrose, Stuart Beedie, Bobby Smith, Grant Jenkins, Bobby Robertson, Jim Bowie and Kenny Thomson took part in the pre-match festivities. The Pars included their former player John Watson and Newcastle included Roy Aitken, Mark McGhee and Paul Sweeney. Norrie received a huge ovation before and after the game.

When I asked him for the reason for asking that the Geordie team be the opponents on such a special evening (they were not the force then they are today), I anticipated a profound answer. With a twinkle in his eye, he replied 'because we knew they were in east Scotland then!' More seriously, he added 'I live for the big atmosphere games, I wanted a game with noise.' The largest roar during the game actually came when, to liven things up, John Watson took a snap shot at goalie Westwater! There was considerable banter among the players which reflected the genuine warmth they all had for the man. Ian McCall, who'd shared a flat with him, told the fans he had smelly feet. Bobby Forrest recalled that at Player of the Year dances, all you could ever aim for was runner up. Pat Stanton said he deserved all he got except for that famous £50 signing on fee. Davie Young said he got nicknamed Hunk because of his performances at preseason training. Finally in their usual devilment his greatest friend John Watson called him big and ugly and having no real bad habits, a bit of a bore! Norrie of course thanked the supporters and his testimonial committee chaired by John Grieve. 'I had taken stick at times but I got a lot of praise too.' One year later came his proudest moment. 'It was a hell of a moment when I led out the team at Hampden in the Skol Cup Final against Hibernian. Scoring the spot kick in the semi-final against Airdrie at Tynecastle was great, though I felt sorry for John who was playing for them. I was really gutted when we lost. That game was definitely there for the taking despite our awful league form.' Despite playing so many matches for the club he claimed he never lost his enthusiasm 'although I hate preseason training. In the last 3 seasons the biggest threat to our Division 1 challenge was ourselves shooting ourselves in the foot, losing games we should have won or drawing too many games.' Of course, I concluded by asking how he saw the future? By January he had already scored 4 vital goals in his 18 games including a particularly memorable last one in the 2–4 win at Dundee. On the playing

Norrie McCathie — Mr Dunfermline

front he told me 'I believe Dunfermline will win promotion this time. I want to lead the club out at one more Cup Final and have another bash at the Premier. I have no intention of going into coaching or playing at a lower level. My businesses are in the town so when I stop playing I'll be coming along to support the team. I genuinely believe Dunfermline will continue to improve. Some say that all a provincial club can win is a Cup. I believe, sincerely, that one day the Athletic can win the Premier League'.

—5—

JOHN WATSON

J ohn Watson was, without doubt, the Athletic's most instantly recognisable celebrity player in the 1980s and yet the club's greatest hero since the days of 'Fergie' came to Dunfermline for a transfer fee of £300, a pint of Special, and a pint of Guinness for his girlfriend. Jim Leishman takes up the story. 'Obviously every generation of Pars fans has their hero, the likes of Dickson or Barry or Fergie but there's no disputing that in the late 1980s, when we went on to win the Division 1 Championship, he was the greatest hero of all. Thousands of youngsters would chant 'John, John, super John' and, as in the days of Roy Barry, opposition fans would give him tremendous stick. And, rather like big Roy, there would be songs at other grounds attacking him even if the Pars were not there, such was the man's stature! I signed him in late 1983 and no manager ever did a better deal yet it was a strange transfer. He had been playing in Hong Kong for the local Rangers where he also had a job as a plumber, but

John Watson in action against Motherwell, October 1987

he hadn't really settled and now he was back in Scotland so, on the recommendation of Andy Young, I went through to the capital, met him in the Cafe-Royal and got him signed up. Frankly there was no suggestion he was to become the great player that he did, he was out of condition and about a stone heavier than his usual 12 and a half stone even though he was 6 foot. His whole career was the sort of story you would find in a kid's comic. You usually hear of players who were outstanding in school or youth football teams or, maybe, they have school boy caps but, as a pupil, at Liberton High in Edinburgh he much preferred to go to Easter Road on a Saturday afternoon. He told me that, if he did get round to playing football, he'd play in goal in Division 7 of the city's amateur league! Well, Willie McFarlane took him to Meadowbank Thistle and he played there 1979–81. What is astonishing is that the towering red haired striker whose height and strength would later install fear into even Premier defences, didn't even score one goal! Once we had him in our first team at Dunfermline, there was little evidence that he'd end up the greatest kid's hero since 'Fergie'. Certainly he got a lot of goals in the second team but he played about 17 games or so in the top team and only ended up with 3 goals. Then the goals began to flow, he got 18 in 1984–85 when we came so close to promotion and 31 in 1985–86 when we went on to win the Second Division Championship.

One of my proudest moments at East End came that evening when he scored his 30th goal of the season against St Johnstone which meant he wrapped up the *Daily Record*'s Golden Shot Trophy and later he'd have his Championship medal. He'd become our greatest scorer since 'Fergie', his grand total was already at 50 and only Sandy McNaughton had done that in the last two decades. In my time at East End he scored 85 about 40 ahead of Ross Jack, what an achievement and Duncan Simpson later told me that meant one goal in every two-and-a-half matches! I was so pleased when, later, he would line up along with Norrie and Craig in the Scotland semi-professional team. When we moved on to Division 1 he still attained 13 strikes but the marking was so much tighter and he contributed a lot despite occasional injuries. Don't forget he also lined up as an effective centre back on occasion and that was an irony as he always declared that his 'pet hate' was a centre back! All in all the club got a heck of a return on their investment. He was in our team photo at the beginning of 1989–90 but I had to be honest and tell him he could not expect so many appearances at that level and John, with his usual frankness, said, look boss, I would rather be remembered by Dunfermline's support for my games when I was at the top and so he decided to leave. Surely there will never be a better memory of John as a player than the goal which gave us the Division 1 flag in May 1989'.

John Watson was also quick to point out the person who contributed so much to his goal tally. He singled out Jim 'Ziggy' Bowie as his favourite player as he depended so much on his regular accurate crosses (he was probably the best since the days of Alex Edwards) and he was 'as furious as the fans' when Jim was allowed to leave in March 1987. 'My main strength was heading the ball. Not only could I time my jump and jump very high I could hang long enough to get the ball, but you needed a good cross.' Bowie too became part of the Par's folklore because, being a real gentleman on the park, he once stopped a promising move against Queen of the South when the defender marking him collapsed with hypothermia! Jim Leishman always claimed that Watson, who was as fearless as his name sake the racing driver, had probably cost £4 a goal'. His goals varied from the ludicrous (John calls his goal at Ayr the best slice since he last played golf) to the brilliant (the flying header from a Beedie corner and Mark Smith flick on which put Rangers out of the Cup) to the golden (the flag winning goal against Meadowbank). In total there were 72 in the league and only Charlie Dickson or Harry Melrose could beat that since the war. John though picks a most unlikely goal as his favourite. 'Jim Bowie sent in a perfectly flighted cross against Montrose, who used to play an extremely effective defensive 5 against us, and I met it with a diving header. The goal against St Johnstone to get the Golden Shot trophy meant a lot to me too. What was especially remark-able about that one was that Norrie actually passed it to me - either that or he miscued it! I also scored with my left foot and that was pretty rare. My other favourites were any I got against

Raith or Cowdenbeath'! Although at times he claims 'he couldn't trap a bag of cement' he also performed well at centre half and it was his ability to switch roles between striker and stopper which led to him winning the B and Q Superskills award in September 1988. Many an ink well has been drained dry as sports writers attempted to analyse the reasons why Dunfermline soared in the late 1980s from the obscurity of Division 2 to the heights of the Premier Division but John Watson, the plumber who could plug a leeky defence and supply goals on tap was surely a major factor.

'When I first came to East End Park, Dunfermline were having a desperate season. Jim had just become the manager and Division 1 football was farthest from my mind, let alone ever playing in the Premier. The club only had three sets of strips and Joe Nelson performed miracles with the training gear, such as it was. Long before I signed, a scout called Ivor Finlayson suggested me to the club and I played as a trialist and scored against Ayr United at Somerset Park. I played up front and got 2, yet I'd played midfield at Meadowbank. Well I think the coach crawled back at 20 mph and I was late for a wedding reception. I thought 'stuff this'. It was a while till I played for the Pars again I can tell you. A few months later I was on the bench when Dunfermline played in the 2–1 Cup defeat at Ibrox which Jim Leishman regards as the game which was, probably, the turning point in the club's fortunes. Jock Wallace admitted later our tactics were completely right and he'd been really worried as he faced the biggest shock since the one he caused at Berwick. At the start of season 1984–85 I was leaner and a lot fitter, and a paltry 1000, I think, turned up to see me hit 4 in a goal romp against Stranraer. We won game after game until a shock league defeat at Ochilview but the game I remember was the Skol Cup defeat by Celtic. I scored both goals in the 2–3 game and the crowd was so large you would have thought you'd gone back in time. Only Celtic's superior fitness took them through. Jim kept roaring instructions from the dug out and got more and more excited until I shouted back at him to calm down'. Those who'd criticised John saying he could only score against weaker opposition had been effectively silenced. The player who hadn't even played a match between the ages of 16–19 was having quite an impact. He admired Joe Jordan and many felt his style of play was remarkably similar. The season ended in disappointment. Despite 18 goals the club was pipped by Montrose and Alloa for promotion. John's best season was, obviously, 1985–86 when he scored 31 goals and the club went on to win the Division 2 flag. 'A major reason why I was scoring so many was the partnership I now had up front with Grant Jenkins. What a dedicated player he was. Despite being part-time he drove one and a quarter hours to and from East End each day and while I got so much credit for getting the goals, I would invariably finish off a move he had instigated and he used to get some terrible knocks making an opening for me. He was a really under rated player.' John won numerous Player of the Match awards and Player of the Year trophies. Jim Leishman recalls 'As 1985–86 began there was a changed atmosphere, a tremendous determination to succeed and a major factor in that was big John who'd just signed a 2 year contract'. 'We did well that autumn and, by November, we were top of the table. Stephen Morrison had become our very own Rivelino with his swerving free kicks, we played St Johnstone who'd been a Premier team only a couple of years earlier and I scored twice in beating them 4–0, we put 6 past Albion Rovers as the goal scoring machine got into top gear, and I scored a brace in a cracking 3–3 local derby with Raith Rovers.

What was remarkable about the Pars fans was that even if you'd scored a good few goals, they would boo a pass back and shout you on to go and get more. I felt they were happier if you'd played well and lost rather than played rubbish and won. They were a very knowledgeable support. They were especially vital at an away game. Well, we knew we were making progress when we had our inevitable Cup tie with Hibernian. We'd played them in the Tom Hart memorial trophy one month before and we took a lot of credit in a 3–5 defeat. I scored twice. I was still part-time and turned down work up at Sullom Voe because it would have meant no football. In the Cup we'd beaten Raith Rovers 2–0. In torrential rain we got a goal in the opening couple of minutes as Jim had preceded it with one of his daft joke telling sessions in the dressing room. Later we put out little Threave 0–5. The Directors watched from the stand i.e., our coach parked beside the wall! We came back in the coach on a freezing cold day and someone put a snowball with a large stone through the window at Dumfries. At Easter Road we did well and Hibs got their largest crowd of the season. I'd to drop into midfield once Dave Moyes got sent off but we only lost 2–0 and we took a lot of encouragement from that display. We were now engaged in a tremendous top of the table battle with Queen of the South and we'd beaten the Division 2 record for unbeaten consecutive games without defeat. It was a proud Pars record'. It was at this time that Roy Woodrow, now the Chairman became a Director and being the owner of a local soft drinks company Jim Leishman could hardly resist telling the media 'he hoped he'd put some fizz into the team'. 'Jim Leishman, of course, was great at fostering team spirit and a good example of that was the 'Pebble Mill' adventure.

Pars fans had adopted 'East Enders' as an unofficial club theme and so club Director Blair Morgan and his son Steven penned their own club lyrics to go with the music and he used his contacts in the music world to get us along to a recording studio in Edinburgh and it was covered on TV by 'Reporting Scotland' Coach Gregor Abel did the B side. Well the BBC at 'Pebble Mill' got to hear about it and millions saw us on UK wide TV with star Anna Wing. Mind you, Jim only got us to learn the words by showing us a soft-porn video on the coach going down and switching it off if we'd not memorised the next verse'! Jim Leishman has other memories of John Watson and team spirit in this period. 'We used to get team spirit by having days out to Powderhall, Gullane, bowling alleys and golf courses. We always stayed in top hotels, gave the players the best meals, travelled in a luxurious coach and had blazers and flannels, all things learned from Jock Stein's day. Well, we'd gone to Gullane for the day, trained at a local park and then played golf. After a meal back at the hotel, Bobby Forrest as usual picked up the golf prizes (either Bobby was great at golf or more likely, he couldn't count!) and then Gregor and I went for a walk. As we came back to the hotel we saw big John mooning at a window. I gave him a good kick I can tell you. He'd a lot of respect for me after that'! 'John is quick to pay tribute to Jim's power of motivation.' He always inspired players to give of their best but players respected the man even if they weren't getting a game in the first team and that is pretty unusual.' In March the Pars had to play 8 games as the backlog of postponed games after an awful winter began to catch up with them but they won 4 and drew 4. A 3–1 defeat at Dumfries was a major set back though. Dunfermline then lost 4–0 at Meadowbank on the evening Hamish McAlpine made a Pars appearance.

'The major factor was that Norrie was suspended and John Hunter has called such an omission 'it was like watching Hamlet without the prince'! Then in mid-April I'll never forget the evening we repeated the 4–0 defeat of St Johnstone. I got several bottles of champagne because the third goal meant I'd got 30 for that season and the Golden Shot award. It was a left foot shot from just outside the box which sealed it and the signing of Gary Thompson who ran the midfield was a boon then too. Gary Thompson, like Davy Moyes, was an inspired Leishman signing. He would bring in players who, while they might not be able to cope in the long term at a higher level, would do a brilliant job in the short-term. His timing was also great. He would sign such players just before the run in and that gave all the players a psychological boost.

On one occasion all the players were at St Andrews preparing for a major game and we all went out for a few drinks one evening. It got dark and we'd to walk across the golf course to get back to the hotel. Well John Donnelly and Gary Thompson both fell into a bunker and were screaming at us but no one could see them. Gary was quite a character'! By this point Queen of the South and Dunfermline remained neck and neck, matching each other stride for stride and the Athletic were doing so well talent scouts were in abundance in the stand. The time of year had come when you watched a match with the tranny pressed against one ear. On April 19th Dunfermline beat East Stirling 4–0 and the fans raced onto the park. At least they were up, but could they take the flag? It was a time of celebration at the club as the 1961 Cup winning team assembled for a dinner dance'.

On the 29th we'd an innocuous 0–0 draw at Ochilview and we knew that Queen of the South led Cowdenbeath 1–3. We'd actually passed their coach on Kincardine bridge. We were all rather deflated as we came off and the disgruntled fans were heading for the exits then the tannoy came out with that 3–3 scoreline, the fans did an about turn and I saw Jim racing with hands outstretched towards Westie, who'd had a great game, before Jim and I were both lofted up and carried by the fans back to the dressing room'. When Dunfermline lost the final game 3–2 at Annfield, the day was best remembered for the incredulity which met Hearts failure to win the Premier Division at Dundee. 'The celebrations at the Paragon club went on into the early hours and it said a lot for Queen of the South that they called to congratulate us. It was just fantastic that we ended up highest goal scorers in Britain! That helped ensure we were the best supported team outwith the Premier'.

'By the time Norrie and I got back form the World Cup in Mexico, Jim had strengthened the team with McCall and Ferguson. Ian was as much into pranks as Norrie and me. From time to time one of the three of us would get scissors out and cut someone's shirt sleeves. Well one day, while all the players were away at training, someone cut Iain Munro's socks so that, when he put them on, his toes went straight through! Munro went ballistic but was delighted he'd finally nailed us. You should have seen his face when Stuart Beedie owned up to the prank. We got off to a good start and we'd a cracker of a Skol Cup tie with St Mirren in a 0–2 defeat in which I was unlucky not to score. We'd a vital 1–2 win at Killie then I scored my goal of the season from a 'Ziggy' cross past Ray Charles in the 1–0 defeat of Montrose and who can forget Norrie's wonderful diving header in a 3–3 draw up at Forfar'? Dunfermline took 18 points in the first quarter but only 11 in the second and John Watson admitted it was much harder to score at this level. 'There were stronger defences and much tighter marking and I only got 13 goals that year. By now the Athletic were not playing with a wide man at all and so the ball did not come down the flanks in the way that it did when 'Ziggy' set up chances for me. Usually when I got the ball I would have my back to goal and at 6 feet, I was up against many central defenders who towered over me, yet I reckon I won about 90% of those high balls. In the early days you have to remember that a lot of defenders did not really know me but now we were playing teams 4 times a season and chances were far fewer. Provided the team was performing well I was not too concerned and I gave 100% in every game. I found it ironic that on occasion Pars fans would shout at me that season. I was dead keen to go full time. By now the Gaffer was and so were a bunch of the young lads, and I felt that Norrie, 'Zico', Ian and I would really benefit from such a move. About this time Crystal Palace came in for me. Gordon McQueen of Airdrie, one of our main rivals rated me highly and told Steve Coppell of Crystal Palace and he came up twice to watch me'. Jim Leishman adds 'A bid came in for £75,000 but the Board decided there was no way it could part with a player so crucial to our challenge and the bid was turned down. It led to the one big argument with John, who felt disappointed he'd not been kept informed, and I felt I learned a lesson. A player involved in transfer speculation had to be kept informed.

From then on I held my breath every time he mentioned there was a vacancy on an oil rig'! John Watson scored in just 90 seconds in November against Queen of the South and then the team pulled off a vital 2–1 win at Dumbarton and 2–2 draw at Morton, the main challengers. 'We all wore 2 strips for the sub zero match at New Year with East Fife and then we took a huge support to the seemingly annual Cup tie at Hibs and new manager Alex Miller. We were not disgraced at all but they took their chances in the 2–0 defeat. That March STV filmed our 1–0 defeat of Dumbarton and commentator Jock Brown told us I hope we'll be filming you in the Premier next time. We were about 7 points clear of second place Morton and when Norrie scored a last minute goal at Clyde, the lad's thoughts were turning to the Championship for all that the Gaffer had told the media, back in August, that the aim this season was to consolidate in Division 1. The cameras came back in March to see us lose a vital game 1–2 to main challengers Morton and I missed a great chance from a McCall cross. Bobby Robertson was so determined to see us get up to the top league but no team had

John Watson savours the 1989 Championship triumph.

won the titles in succession. Archie MacPherson of the BBC felt maybe we were suffering from stage fright. There was no lack of nerves when we lost to Brechin 0–2 but at least Morton lost too. We finally won promotion at the end of April although we only beat Queen of the South 1–0 after they put up a grandstand finish and I was unlucky not to settle it in the second half when I was put clear and only had the goalie to beat. We threw Mr Rennie and the Gaffer in the bath and had a great night in the Paragon and East Port bars. We also had the reward of a holiday in Majorca. We went to Airdrie knowing we could still get the flag. Leish opened the dressing room door, said listen to the Pars support, just go for it but we lost 2–1 and I got an elbow in the face in the opening minute. I didn't play in the last game as I was injured'.

John admits he found season 1987–88 difficult in the Premier Division yet he reserved his best games for matches against Rangers and Terry Butcher and Hearts and Dave McPherson.

'You simply could never make a mistake at all at that level, there was never time to get the ball under control or look around where you were going to play it. If you ever made an error it was pounced on. Defences were big, powerful and so well organised and much more skilful. I was not all that fit in the autumn and didn't get into the team till the October when I scored in the 2–1 defeat of Morton and 2–0 of St Mirren then there was the other problem, the calibre of goalies at that level. It was going to be a difficult season despite the arrival of Graeme and Craig Robertson and, later, Bobby and Mark Smith, Billy Kirkwood and John Holt. Early on we had good results including beating Celtic 2–1 and the 3–3 draw with Hibs and 0–1 win at Hibs in which I played. However the match I could never forget was the sensational win over Rangers in the Cup. We'd got a pleasant break from the league when we met Ayr in the Cup and put them out away 0–2 after a 1–1 home draw. We came out of the hat with Rangers and the media promptly wrote us off completely. We were to be sacrificial lambs. The Gaffer took us up to St Andrew's and the feeling in the camp was that they might under estimate us. The Gaffer, meanwhile, subjected us to a reading of 'David and Goliath'! The team was: McKellar, G Robertson, McCathie, Holt, Anderson, C Robertson, Beedie, R Smith, M Smith, Watson, Jack and subs: Ferguson and Kirkwood. The game was fast and furious from the whistle but what a boost we got when Mark got on the end of a Craig pass, he avoided the offside trap, left Jan Bertram for dead and lofted that incredible cross which left goalie Chris Woods stranded as the ball flew over his head into the net. Mark tried to tell us later in the dressing room that he had meant it! John Brown was sent off and later my goal was the product of the training ground. Stuart took the corner, Mark flicked it backwards to the near post and I dived in and sent a beaut of a header screaming into the net. We were put under enormous pressure but we coped. They gave Mark a 'superfit' award and the lad collapsed through exhaustion'! Dunfermline lost in the next round at Hearts but, despite some good results at the tail of the season, the Pars were relegated in the Celtic centenary game.

'In 1988–89 I made 35 appearances in the Championship

season and I scored 16 goals but the one in the final game on 13th May against Meadowbank was, obviously, the most important. Ross Jack scored 18 and we formed an effective strike partnership. We began the season beating Motherwell 2–1 and losing 1–4 to Hearts in the Skol Cup which whetted our appetite for a quick return but in that latter game I blazed an easy chance over the bar early on. We beat Raith 2–1 in the derby match and beat Killie 3–0 and Airdrie 1–0. However, we lost 2–1 at Brockville and we all felt Falkirk were the main threat and so it proved. In a game with Queen of the South I got 'Man of the Match' yet played in defence as Norrie was sidelined. I'd scored 7 in my first 10 games but we hit a bad patch in October and November with too many draws until we got 2 vital points in a 0–1 win at St Johnstone, a team always packed with many former Pars players. We were to win 8 of the next 9 matches. At the turn of the year I scored twice in the 5–1 defeat of Ayr and that was followed by a memorable 3–0 defeat of local rivals Falkirk at Hogmanay before a 12,889 crowd. Ross got 2, I got the other. The crowd at that game was phenomenol. Our fans had faces painted black and white and the Falkirk ones blue and white. At one point I felt they should have stopped the match to allow the players to watch the fans! Duncan Simpson set me a target as I now had 80 goals for the club. I would have needed 7 more to catch Bert Paton'.

It was about this time that physio Philip Yeates quit show-business and Sigourney Weaver's thighs on a film set in Kenya to concentrate on the crocks in the treatment room at East End. 'We did doubt his sanity' says big Jim. By now John had completed his 200th career appearance. Falkirk was not the only big game. 'The Cup is always a welcome break from the stress of the league and we met Aberdeen in the Cup. The Gaffer took us to Dunblane Hydro and tried to psyche out Alex Smith because, every time the media turned up, the TV only saw us lazing around to give the impression we were not taking the match too seriously. Well we drew 0–0 before 16,656 and no one could believe the saves Theo Snelders had that day from Ross. We lost the replay 3–1 up at Pittodrie'. Things seemed to be going really smoothly as the Pars had a good run of consecutive wins 'but then we'd 2 really bad results. We lost 4–0 at Falkirk and 0–1 at home to Raith. Jim Duffy's team had won just 3 games in the last 12 when they met us and they regarded the match with us as a last chance saloon. After some disappointing draws we got back on tracks when Dave Irons scored a screamer to win 0–1 at Forfar and it was an enjoyable drive home especially as Falkirk had come to grief at Airdrie. We thought we might win the flag one week early but I scored in a disappointing 1–1 draw with Clyde which was not enough. 13th May was a real red letter day. The nerves were bad and they got a whole lost worse when Meadowbank scored. Then I remember Graeme Robertson hit a long ball down the right, Boyd failed to cut it out and I drew Jim McQueen and slotted it home. As news came through that things had not gone to plan for Falkirk up at Forfar some of the pressure evaporated. It was a great night as we went off to Cagneys, the East Port bar, Pitbauchlie and Noddy's Neuk. Bobby Smith was presented with the Cup and I'll never forget the laps of honour and what that Division 1 Championship meant to the support and the town. It was so strange, subsequently, to play against the Pars for Airdrie in the Skol Cup Semi-Final and directly in opposition to Norrie, my best friend. I never slept for 3 nights before that game. It meant so much to Norrie to win it. I would have loved to play another 2 years at East End but, really, I was a good Division 1 player and I knew well my limitations. Today I rarely go to Pars games. I am hopeless at just watching a game, as I was then.'

—6—

CHARLIE DICKSON

It was the 88th minute of the Scottish Cup Final replay on Wednesday 26th April 1961 at Hampden, where the game had kicked off at 6.15 pm as Queen's Park did not yet have floodlights. It was a dark, grey evening and the rain poured down but the 87,660 crowd knew the Athletic were seconds away from a famous victory as they held on desperately to their hard fought 1–0 lead. Alec Smith chipped forward nothing more than an optimistic lob. Charlie Dickson went off on a token chase for the long ball, which was surely Frank Haffey's all the way. Suddenly, inexplicably, Haffey clutched it, then dropped it. It fell neatly at the feet of Charlie Dickson and the Athletic forward, who scored a post-war record 157 league goals, ran one of the simplest ever over the goal line. Dunfermline had their first major trophy, and anyone who has ever sat in the Jock Stein lounge at East End knows the famous scene where the large white raincoated manager made a dash from the dug-out for his goalie. Eddie Connachan was carried shoulder high by his mates off the pitch and, later, Billy McNeill of Celtic said 'He broke our hearts more than any goalie I have ever seen'! The Athletic captain Ron Mailer added 'I have never seen a display of goalkeeping to match what we have witnessed tonight'. As for Charlie Dickson, he was now a Pars immortal. It is a paradox then that vast numbers of Pars fans today have probably neither seen nor heard of one of the club's greatest heroes, yet the former chat show host and sports columnist Michael Parkinson has probably put his finger on a general reason why. Parkinson needs little excuse to bring into a sports article mention of his home town team, Barnsley FC and one particularly robust (a euphemism if ever there was one) defender called Skinner Normanton. Tales of Skinner's ferocious tackling got the better with each and every telling and all the more exaggerated till people began to enquire whether the

Charlie Dickson, a legend with Dunfermline fans

Columnist's hero from childhood had even existed or was it all a good story? 'You have to remember' says Parkinson 'that even in the 1960's there was a discernible link for fans with the past but today if you tell the fans about the players of 40 or 50 years ago, they come across not so much as ghostly characters on a distant landscape but as creatures from another planet'! It would have been tempting to include in this book whole chapters on the likes of Andy Wilson and Bobby Skinner, but if the 3 aims were to relive the 1996 Championship triumph, to highlight Norrie's wonderful contribution and to focus on some of the greatest stars since the halcyon days of the 1960s then they did not fit the criteria. If now we have come to a player whom many at East End never saw or whom some, like John Hunter, feel did not have a shot worthy of the name, and certainly was anything but a tricky player, then I make no apology. He surpassed the scoring record of Bobby Skinner in 1959–60, his double hat-trick against St Mirren in 1961 broke the striker's record at the club, he was enthusiastic and tenacious, and lethal with those long legs in the box and was very nippy. He scored 19 Scottish Cup goals but that soft one in April 1961 should have given him the freedom of the city!

From the very beginning you could see that Portobello born Charlie had something special. An electrician, he was playing for Penicuik Athletic when Bobby Ancell of Dunfermline spotted him and he scored 2 of the Pars' 3 goals on his debut at Stenhousemuir in January 1955. He was signed to replace the club's top scorer Millar, who'd gone to Rangers and paid off the club's overdraft into the bargain. By April, the club was in the headlines for 2 reasons. The Pars were promoted from Division 2 as runners up to Airdrie and they told the Scottish league they thought it was not a good idea to allow TV cameras into grounds! Had they been admitted, they would have noticed that Charlie had a full head of hair yet, at his peak in 1961, the fans used to shout at him 'chalk your cue Charlie', according to veteran fan Alex Fawcett, if his bald pate failed to connect with the ball! The following season he got off to a good start. There was a new manager Andy Dickson, and he was responsible for bringing Peebles from Falkirk. 'We made a good start to the league but we couldn't sustain it and we were in mid-table at the year's end. I couldn't always play because of national service commitments. In fact I'd be away all week with the RAF and I'd only get back for the game. You could go for days with no real training at all. We would have been relegated but for some fabulous wins that April including our 1–0 mid-week victory over the Champions Rangers'. The following year Dunfermline were relegated in the final game then one year later they came straight back, these being the famous yo yo years. They were promoted as runners up to Stirling and scored an astonishing 120 goals in the process, much of this success was due to Charlie who scored 40 goals including an astonishing 4 hat-tricks!

1958–59 proved a desperate struggle back in the top division despite striker Harry Melrose being enticed from Rangers. Success in the Cup (they reached Round 4) could not make up for abysmal failure in the league but older fans will never forget how that season ended on Saturday 18th April. 'We went into our last game on 26 points in equal 2nd bottom spot with Falkirk but they had a better goal average' he recalls. 'Falkirk were held to a draw at Brockville by Raith and Rangers free transfer man Harry Melrose went on to hit 6 goals in an incredible 10–1 win over Partick Thistle! *The Sunday Mail* said 'the architect of this prodigious feat was often maligned home centre-forward Charlie Dickson. With 5 assists and one goal, he had the Thistle defence running round in circles and finished the half as the greatest Dunfermline benefactor since Andrew Carnegie. Inspired by Dickson's brilliant leadership, the entire Dunfermline team rose to football brilliance.' Dunfermline hoped in 1959–60 to get established in Division 1 and Andy Dickson signed George Miller and Cammy Fraser. By the end of 1959, with the team failing to win even one away game, it was obvious they faced their usual struggle. The manager resigned after a humiliating Cup exit at the hands of Stenhousemuir.

On 14th March 1960 Jock Stein became manager. 'It has become part of the club folklore that he guided us to 6 consecutive wins in our last games of the season and we ended up safely in mid-table. Four days after he arrived we beat his old club Celtic at East End 3–2 and I scored in the first 10 seconds. Then I scored after 40 seconds in a 0–2 win at St Mirren. He did not make any new signings, he carried on with the players Mr Dickson had left him but he coached us to play as a team and we never looked back.' Bob Crampsey in *Mr Stein* (1986) pointed out that the burly new manager concentrated on the Pars defence 'there was no point having an umbrella if your boots let in water' he used to say. Charlie takes up the story 'we all knew the tricky one was going to be the next one at home to Killie as they were going great guns, were second in the table and had a Cup Semi-Final place. Mr Stein demanded that the postponed league game go ahead on the following Monday as the Ayrshire lads would still have their minds on the Cup Final. Against all the odds we pulled it off 1–0. Mr Stein's psychology clearly worked though he'd had to badger the Directors into doing it'. With wins over Airdrie 1–0, Clyde 3–1 and Stirling Albion 4–1 Athletic supporters hailed Stein's start as a miracle triumph, Bob Crampsey states significantly 'he had the definite advantage that everyone expected the club to go down. Division 2 seemed their natural habitat.' Stein knew well that however willing or enthusiastic his charges were, they needed to be reinforced. He wanted an end to the annual flirtation with relegation. He brought in Willie Cunningham, Tommy McDonald, Dan McLindon, Willie Callaghan and Jackie Sinclair. 'He also had to change our thinking' Charlie points out 'we ended up going to Ibrox, Parkhead and Pittodrie expecting to win - an outrageous thought one year or two before. All the same, he reminded us our aim was to get established in the first division—it was not the flag or Cup; at least, not yet'! Dunfermline were never in any danger of relegation in 1960–61, they ended up in a comfortable mid-table position.

Charlie had another outstanding season in the league scoring 18 goals compared to his 25 in 1960, 14 in 1959. He was top scorer but it was the 4 in the Cup which would prove so significant despite his 2 consecutive hat-tricks against Motherwell (4–2) and Dundee (4–2) in October and 6 other doubles. 'I have often been asked in recent years, didn't my goalscoring attract bids from larger clubs but if so, the Board weren't going to tell me. You didn't have the endless media speculation in those days.' There was little suggestion of the glory to come, in January 1961, when the Athletic set out on the Cup trail by beating Berwick Rangers in England 1–4, Dickson scoring the equaliser. Playing on the tight, bumpy pitch in front of a small crowd at Stranraer was no easier in 1961 than it is 35 years later but Charlie scored another vital goal in a comfortable 1–3 victory. 'Some felt our luck had run out when we were drawn to meet Aberdeen, up at Pittodrie who'd played in the Final two years earlier. Mr Stein took us up there the night before because he was determined to make us feel like a big team which had ambitions.' Scottish Football sat up and took notice when the Athletic came away with a startling 3–6 scoreline. A Dickson cross gave Smith the equaliser and he scored the goal that made it 2–1. It was a fine display of attacking football masterminded by a man who'd learned from the Hungarians about coaching one year earlier. Jock Stein's prayer that he'd get a much easier home fixture was granted and Dunfermline moved smoothly to the dizzy heights of the Semi-Final beating Alloa 4–0. 'We could now really concentrate on the Cup Semi-Final with St Mirren at Tynecastle because home league wins over Partick and St Johnstone 5–1, in which I scored, meant we no longer had any concerns about our league safety.' On 1st April 10,000 Fife fans were in the 31,930 crowd making the volume of noise that would become the Pars hallmark in years to come but, despite that, the score remained 0–0. *The Scottish Sunday Express* said 'Peebles and Melrose were clever wingers but Charlie Dickson was the main threat down the middle.'

'That was up until about 10 minutes into the second half when Peebles hit a high ball into the goalmouth, I went for it with Clunie and got my header in but he crashed into me and I was stretchered off'. 16,741 attended the replay. Dunfermline won deservedly, being the superior team yet the goal came when, in a dour dreich affair, Harry Melrose hit a shot in the 67th minute off Paisley defender Stewart. Charlie wasn't able to play. 'It was an honour to have made our first Scottish Cup Final but to win it would mean somehow defeating Celtic who'd only won it 17 times! Mr Stein used his psychological approach by kitting us out in blazers and flannels so at least we looked the part and then he booked us all in at the Seamill Hydro to make us feel upsides with Celtic. He was furious with us when we lost 6–0 to Clyde in a run of the mill end of the season affair. It was poor preparation for the biggest game of our lives. Meanwhile the town had gone daft in preparation for the big day. All the shop windows displayed the famous black and white colours and there were team photos everywhere.'

On April 22nd the whole of Scotland and certainly the huge 113,328 crowd expected Celtic to win the Cup against a team without appendicitis-stricken McDonald. Then the Pars lost Williamson with an early injury. The ten men (no subs in 1961) held Celtic at bay. The Pars played out of their skins, were first to every tackle and behind them was goalkeeping sensation Eddie Connachan after all. 'We almost scored in the first minute. I took the ball up the left with Harry, he got it to Peebles who let go a fierce shot and briefly it squirmed out of Haffey's grasp but a Celtic defender hooked it clear.' The media now agreed that a Provincial club only gets one bite at the cherry. Celtic would finish off the job in midweek. Bob Crampsey adds that Mr Stein did not subscribe to this piece of folk wisdom. He knew Celtic as well as anyone. He suspected that the pressure would be heavy on Celtic who'd won nothing in four long years. In addition, Dunfermline had not been overawed in that first game and Stein felt they'd done enough to win. The team for the replay was: Connachan, Fraser, Cunningham, Mailer, Miller, Sweeney, Peebles, Smith, Thomson, Dickson and Melrose. 'I was moved to inside left with David Thomson playing centre-forward. Mr Stein left out Williamson and McLindon, George Miller wore no. 5 and Sweeney was simply told to mark Willie Fernie. He never left him all night! Our goal was under constant siege on an awful wet evening but Eddie's handling of the greasy ball was magnificent. He had the Celtic forwards in despair as he saved from Gallacher, Hughes and Chalmers'. Then Dunfermline, who had contrived precisely one chance in the first half, scored in the teeth of relentless Celtic pressure and the scorer was Thomson who hadn't even played in the first game. Peebles screamed down the left, left Mackay for dead, got in his cross but it was deflected off a Celtic head to Davie Thomson, who was standing totally unmarked in the centre of the penalty area. He met it perfectly with a brilliant flick of the head and beat Haffey all ends up. The Dunfermline end simply erupted as Celtic's support realised they really were in a game. Celtic roared back and Bob Crampsey later described Connachan 'as a goalie guarding his net like a man possessed'.

Everyone waited for the fumble that would give it to Celtic as their forwards surrounded his goal like bees to a honey pot but the fumble, when it came was at the other end and Charlie just could not believe his luck! *The Scottish Daily Express* commented 'Inside left Charlie Dickson has been a great servant for Dunfermline and he made certain of their moment of glory with that 88th minute goal. The Dunfermline players danced with joy'. All the way back to Fife people were standing out in the rain to cheer the jubilant convoy of players and fans home. They had won the 76th Cup Final in their own 76th year. At the town boundary the players got into the open topped bus and a local band (playing 'The Happy Wanderer' over and over again) preceded them in triumph to the balcony at the City chambers. There, thousands of people and the TV cameras awaited them. Charlie recalls 'the noise, the welcome, and that atmosphere will live with me forever'. Jock Stein said 'I have great memories of winning the European Cup with Celtic but no memory was greater than that night at Dunfermline'. Arthur Montford later recalled 'it was one of the great nights for Scotsport'. Chairman David Thomson added 'we intend to remain at the top and to build a stadium where we'll have the facilities to bring the top European teams to Dunfermline'. Veteran fan Alex Fawcett recalls that one of the main souvenirs was a black and white 'cup winning ashtray', which would not be appropriate in the 'politically correct' 1990s! Meanwhile Charlie remained the club's top goalscorer in 1961–62. He scored 29 in total, 16 league, 5 in the Cup and now, significantly, 5 in Europe. A feature of Dunfermline Athletic in the next decade would be those bitterly cold dark winter evenings when the saltire flew proudly over the new stand and thousands packed into the ground to watch stirring battles against the cream of Europe. Only Rangers and the two clubs in the capital preceded the Fifers at this level.

For a club whose idea of playing abroad was going to Berwick and who previously only got into Europe if there was a war on, this was a whole new ball game. Dunfermline were now to meet the cream but you always get a few clots in cream and the baptism came against the part-timers St Patrick's Athletic of Dublin. Dunfermline's squad now included the names of Paton, Lunn and Thomson and 10,000 watched them comfortably win 4–1. Charlie scored at the 3–1 stage and got 2 more in an away 0–4 second leg romp. 'When we met Vardar of Skopje in Yugoslavia in the next round it was our first real taste of continental football and we were not that impressed as it took a complex 48 hour trip to get to Macedonia. We won 5–0 in the first leg at home and I scored twice having been dropped in the previous league game. We took command from the start and I scored the second when I met a cross from Melrose. Just on half-time I beat their centre-half to the jump to get on to a lob from Miller and I ran on to head the ball as it bounced, past their goalie. We lost the ferocious second leg 2–0 in a game which was all one way but Mr Stein's defensive tactics and, of course, Eddie Connachan saw us through.' There had been a poor start to the league but the Pars hit form at the turn of the year and enjoyed 12 games without defeat. On 30th December 1961 before a 5,153 crowd, Dunfermline defeated St Mirren 7–0 at home. Charlie hit his memorable double hat-trick. 'I remember I ended up with the yellow coloured ball because the pitch was totally covered in snow. I think I was getting my own back for the cup Semi-Final injury'. Meanwhile the players were built up at the prospect of a Quarter-Final tie in the European Cup Winners Cup though Bob Crampsey found that Jock Stein confided that all his European targets for 1961–62 had already been met. In mid-February the Athletic came out of the hat with Ujpesti Dozsa of Hungary. The Pars put up a gallant effort in Budapest only going down there 4–3 which increased confidence for the second leg. 24,000 paid to watch the Athletic go out 0–1. 'In many ways the season was actually better than the previous one. We'd reached that Quarter-Final, get a best ever 4th place in the league which ensured our place in Europe and were narrowly defeated 1–0 away to St Mirren in the Scottish Cup Quarter-Final. The new stadium was now in place and the floodlighting updated'. In 1962–63 Charlie was to score only 13 goals and none of them in Europe and that is all the more remarkable given that the season is now remembered for 2 of the greatest games of the period against the Bank of England team Everton and Spanish cracks Valencia. 'Who are Dunfermline' the Merseyside manager Catterick enquired as the teams came out of the hat? He was soon to learn. Few gave the Pars a chance in the away tie but 40,240 saw the Athletic go down 1–0 in a match they called robust or, in England, dirty. 25,000 watched the return and Charlie played in both, the line ups being the same.

'George Miller scored in the opening minutes and we were all square. Harry Melrose sealed a famous night from a suspiciously offside position'. In Round 2 it seemed hopeless when Fairs Cup holders Valencia raced to a 4–0 lead. However, Charlie was dropped for the sensational second leg as Jock Stein wanted to experiment with the precocious teenage wingers Edwards and Sinclair. It is well documented that amidst total pandemonium the Pars pulled them back 6–6 only to lose on a neutral venue. Bob Crampsey recalls commentating on the match and not being able to hear his own voice in the last half hour. More players were now arriving notably Tommy Callaghan and Jim McLean. In the Scottish Cup they went out 1–3 to St Mirren in Round 3 and in the league the Pars ended up mid-table as Jock Stein tried every permutation. Charlie did score in the Fife Cup Final, the only trophy an entertaining season produced. 1963–64 would be Charlie's last at the club yet he was to score 20 goals and end up second highest scorer. There were to be no European distractions that season and they made a good start with 5 wins and 2 draws in the opening 7. Charlie scored in the opening 2–0 home defeat of Motherwell and cracked in 4 League Cup goals. However, hopes of the flag died over a poor New Year period. In the Cup he put 5 past Fraserburgh in an easy Round 2 win, Round 3 was similar as they trounced East Stirling 6–1.

By the time Charlie scored his hat-trick in the 7–0 home thrashing of Ayr United in the Quarter-Final, Jock Stein had gone. Bob Crampsey, his biographer, has said that 'It is no great criticism to say that there was an element of self-interest in the move. The nature of football management is such that it makes very good sense to move while they are on the up swing'. The timing certainly was strange, even his destination was not disclosed, though later one learned it would be to Hibs. 'The Cup winning team was now breaking up and there was a feeling of unease at the club. We were drawn to meet Rangers in the Cup Semi-Final and that only added to the disappointment as they were set to win the league so a place in the Final against them would have meant qualification for the Cup Winners Cup'. Stein took the team to Dunblane Hydro to prepare, elected to have Charlie head the attack as he'd already accumulated 8 Cup goals in the competition, and then lost McLean with a bad injury. The match, which Rangers won 1–0, was not one to remember, the Pars lost their way and the ball rarely reached Smith or Dickson who were now visibly slower. At season's end the Pars were a commendable 5th but Charlie only had 8 of the 64 league goals scored and, come the close season, new manager Willie Cunningham brought in Ferguson, McLaughlin and Kilgannon to score goals. The writing was on the wall especially as he had a troublesome injury and in the autumn of 1964 Charlie left East End. 'I went to Queen of the South for £2,150 and one year later I actually played against the Pars in a Round 1 Cup tie. I wanted to score against my old pals but it was not to be. Dunfermline won 0–2. A year later I went to Australia'. By October 1964 he had been over 9 years at East End. His goals tally, including those eleven hat-tricks, will surely never be equalled. He was an inspirational Pars forward, arguably the best ever, and, even today at East End, if the Pars are in trouble, you will hear one of the older fans shout out 'send for Charlie'! 'I always watch for the Dunfermline score on a Saturday and I really enjoyed the Centenary celebrations in 1985 as I'd lost touch with a lot of my old mates. I also played with Bert Paton and it is just fantastic what he has achieved'. Today he lives quietly in Dunbar.

—7—

ALEX FERGUSON

If you want to work out the age of a Dunfermline Athletic supporter, then just ask who their Pars favourites were. When they reply Andy Wilson, Bobby Skinner, Gerry Mays, Charlie Dickson, Roy Barry, Sandy McNaughton, John Watson or Norrie McCathie you can probably pin down the correct era. If a chapter on Charlie Dickson is an excuse to relive the 1961 Cup Final or Pat Gardner the 1968 one, then Alex Ferguson should have brought back memories of 1965 but Dunfermline's highest goalscorer was not selected. 'I scored 21 that year and 39 in 1965–66 and 29 in 1966–67 after which I moved for the then club record fee of £60,000 to Rangers but that was, without doubt, the most disappointing episode in my whole playing career. Despite that, I actually got on well with manager Willie Cunningham. We'd a sort of love/hate relationship but, in the main, I respected him because he was honest and that is important in a manager.' If Rab Butler was the greatest Prime Minister Britain never had, then Alex Ferguson was the greatest Athletic Cup Winner we were not allowed to see. Alex, who had played in the 2–0 Cup Semi-Final win over Hibernian at Tynecastle in a forward line comprising Edwards, Smith, Ferguson, Melrose and Sinclair, was replaced by McLaughlin in the Cup Final and it was he who put the Pars 2–1 up at half-time. Alex had scored the previous Saturday in the disappointing 1–1 draw at home to St Johnstone, which effectively sealed all hopes of the Flag but, in a season when he was top scorer with those 21 goals, it was the only one he'd scored in the previous dozen games. For all that, Alex Ferguson, one of the biggest names in football in Europe, far less Scotland, has fond memories of his time at East End. 'I used to get picked up in Airdrie in the club van by George Miller, Jim Herriot and Jim McLean, who came from the Wishaw and Larkhall area and, between them, they were responsible for the care and driving of it. There was always a lot of leg pull and banter on the way in and their laughs were just great. We would invariably stop on the way for egg butties and arrive late on the training ground which had Mr Cunningham somewhat less than pleased.'

Former Queens Park player Alex Ferguson was, surely one of the shrewdest investments any Pars manager ever made. Alex came from Govan. 'My background gave me a passion for football and taught me the importance of football and community. In my days up at St Johnstone I was an apprentice toolmaker and a shop steward. Today I am rather more financially secure - but I am still the guy I ever was.' He scored 66 league goals putting him behind only Dickson 157, Melrose 73, Watson 72 and Smith 67 and he came to the Athletic from St Johnstone. 'I was playing for the Saints but not really enjoying it, so it was just perfect when I learned that Bobby Brown and Willie Cunningham had arranged a swap deal. Dunfermline were obviously a great club thanks to the transformation Jock Stein had brought about. The club was certainly in transition in the summer of 1964 and I came along with John Kilgannon who signed from Ayr United, and John McLaughlin from Millwall. Mr Cunningham was certainly determined to increase the club's fire power! Dan McLindon took my place up at Perth. Jock Stein had left Tommy and Willie Callaghan, my great friend Bert, Alex Edwards, Jackie Sinclair, Eric Martin and John Lunn. Of course, many of the famous 1961 Cup Winning side had now gone. When I was there it was an excellent team, full of characters and there was a great team spirit. I can still remember the fun of going on holiday with Alex Smith, Jackie Sinclair and John Grieve (East Port bar). It didn't matter who you were playing, those guys gave it everything. I scored a lot of goals for Dunfermline in my three years but the first came on a tour of Ireland in the August then I scored in a 1–4 win in the League Cup at Airdrie. I scored three in three games and for once, we qualified from our section but lost in the Quarter-Final to Rangers. You never forget your first hat-trick either and mine came in a 7–2 victory over Clyde one month later.'

As hopes in the League Cup dissolved, Dunfermline embarked

Alex Ferguson scores with a header against Hearts

on their Fairs Cup campaign against Orgryte of Sweden. 'I didn't play in the first leg which we won 4–2 but I played in the 0–0 draw in Gothenberg at a ground which later in life on 11th May 1983 would mean rather more to me'! Round 2 was against Stuttgart and in the 1–0 home victory Ferguson harassed the German keeper all evening. His 'rummel them up' style, where a defence tried to mix it with the Athletic attack, would have been ideal in the 1965 Cup Final. The Fifers held on in the second leg 0–0 in a match now remembered for Jim Herriot's penalty save in the dying minutes. 'Memories of those cold mid week evenings in Europe are just magic even now. I can think back to the team trooping out on to the pitch and, as you looked at the compact family enclosures on either side you could see dotted around the familiar face of pals and opponents from clubs like Hearts and Hibernian!

Youngsters today probably have no concept of the extent to which Dunfermline, 30 years ago, had become a major force in Europe. We were playing there even before Celtic! Alex Ferguson remembers the next game well. 'At the end of the year we pulled off a notable first. We beat them 2–1, Jackie getting the other one. One month later we'd to go to Spain for the Quarter-Final of the Fairs Cup and, though we lost 1–0, we'd the rare experience of being applauded off the park by the huge Bilbao support. Mr Cunningham played the team which, on the Saturday, had beaten Motherwell 3–1 at Fir Park. We played the same attacking formation in Bilbao and the locals booed their own team! What a welcome we were to receive on our return at Turnhouse. We won the second leg 1–0 and I'd a goal chalked off but we lost the eventual play off.' While Dunfermline made solid progress on a European stage, fixtures began to pile up and the media began to wonder whether the Athletic could pull off the Treble or at least the Double! Dunfermline were probably at the height of their powers. They would conclude 1965 with 121 goals in all competitions, 1966 with 131.

Alex along with John McLaughlin, Jackie Sinclair, Harry Melrose and Alex Smith would all end up in double figures. By the time they played Bilbao they were already second in the league and had put Queen of the South 2–0, Airdrie 3–1 and Third Lanark 4–2 out of the Cup. 'We met Third Lanark in a Cup replay at neutral venue namely Tynecastle and I scored twice and we went back there for the Semi-Final to meet Hibs. Over 30,000 were packed in that day in late March and, as the fans walked up from Haymarket station, the papers' headlines prophesied an all-green final. Celtic were playing Motherwell in the other Semi. It was, beyond any doubt, the most memorable match for me as a Dunfermline player. We were on a high because, days earlier, we'd put 8 past Third Lanark at home! Harry scored in the first half, Alex in the second and Hibs had no answer to the attacking formation Mr Cunningham utilised. Our team was Herriot, Callaghan and Lunn, Thomson, McLean, T Callaghan, Edwards, Smith, Ferguson, Melrose and Sinclair. Alex and Harry acted as linkmen all afternoon and supplied all the ammunition we needed to make our second Final in a mere 4 years. Meanwhile the contest at the top of the table would be envied today as we battled it out with Kilmarnock, Hearts, Hibs and Rangers. A few days later we lost a crucial game 1–0 at Hibs as they took revenge but we won our next 3 home games and that set us up for a match at East End against lowly St Johnstone. Our goal average was better than Kilmarnock's, who would go on to pip Hearts at Tynecastle, so it could be argued that a win in this game would have given us the title. St Johnstone got their goal from an offside position, I equalised from a John Lunn pass but we just lacked the composure to finish it. Dunfermline lost a classic Cup Final 3–2. I was sitting in the stand! Mr Cunningham had told the players the team about half an hour before the Cup Final. There was little consolation in beating Celtic 5–1 in the league in the last match of 1964–65.'

'In 1965–66 I recall the usual team was Martin, Callaghan, Lunn, Smith, McLean, T Callaghan, Edwards, Paton, Fleming, Ferguson and Robertson, along with Melrose and Thomson. By now I was developing not only as a player but learning from the manager the skills I would need later in my career. As a manager I feel the main influences on me were Cunningham, Jock Stein and, later on, Scot Symon. We would sit for hours in those days and talk football, usually in the Regal Restaurant with Bertie, Willie, Jim, Hugh and George. Mr Cunningham encouraged you to go out on the pitch, play your normal game and express yourself and so the players got on with it themselves. Maybe that is an indictment of modern management. However, Mr Cunningham complemented that with his ability to sign outstanding players like Roy Barry or Jim Fleming or Martin. The players used to concoct complex freekicks among themselves and I can remember the satisfaction it gave me to score one against Celtic involving Alex, Bertie, Pat Delaney and me after Billy McNeill, my neighbour in Glasgow, had said Celtic knew every routine we could think up'! Alex Ferguson had a devastating season in 1965–66 scoring a record 31 league goals and 39 in total. The team's total amounted to a breathtaking 131! 'And Bertie was second on 25'. In the August I got a hat-trick against St Johnstone, another in the October against Partick Thistle. I'd 22 goals by the time we pulled off the rare 2–3 win at Ibrox on Christmas day. That season we got a bye into Round 2 of the Inter Cities Fairs Cup and then met Danish team Boldklub. We won the first leg comfortably 5–0 and then won away 2–4. I got the last one from a Robertson corner which Bertie headed on to me'. The goal summed up Alex's most deadly skill - that of a finisher. He did not have a particularly hard shot nor could he dribble but he was lethal with his close control, his ability to turn and in the penalty box he just didn't miss. 'An example of the size of crowds in those days was the 8,000 who turned up on a bitter evening to see us play Dukla Prague. I scored twice but it was a friendly - a testimonial for Ronnie Mailer'. That Christmas, Pars fans celebrated a result they couldn't believe. Alex Ferguson earned a rave review as Dunfermline beat Rangers 2–3 at Ibrox! 'Our away win in Norway was our first on the continent and now we met crack Czech team Spartak Brno. Bertie and I scored to give us a crucial 2–0 lead. We drew the away leg 0–0 after an endless journey. We also scored twice apiece in the cup Round 2 against Stirling in a 4–1 win having beaten Partick earlier 3–1. The Quarter-Final was a cracker. We beat Kilmarnock 2–1 with Alex Edwards scoring the fantastic winner in the last minute. We'd high hopes in the league but consecutive defeats in March ended that. Then we lost 2–0 in the Cup Semi-Final to Celtic at Ibrox.' Early in the game Ian Hunter seemed to have brilliantly headed the Pars into the lead but as Ronnie Simpson scooped the ball out of the net Ref Hugh Philips claimed that Fergie had pushed a defender out of the way. Alex ran all afternoon but it was not to be. By the time of the Fairs Cup Quarter-Final Alex had scored another hat-trick, against St Johnstone in a 5–1 win at home. 'Bertie gave us a goal at the death in the first leg of the Quarter-Final against Real Zaragoza then we were in Spain just 4 days after the exertions in the Cup Semi-Final. We went down 4–2 after extra time as away goals did not yet count double in the event of a draw. I scored in the last minute of the game and again in extra time and we got a standing ovation as we came off'. In the league the Athletic scored their highest ever total of goals and Fergie had even beaten Charlie Dickson's enviable record. 'I was helped by the fact I scored 7 in just 2 games that April. I then put in a transfer request but I was turned down. I was wanting a new contract.'

Alex Ferguson doesn't hesitate in recalling the 2 most memorable games he was ever involved in. 'They both came in my last season at East End in 1966–67 ie the unbelievable 5–6 match with Hibs and the equally outstanding 4–5 defeat by Celtic. I have discussed this with Bert and I know he still singles them out too as, I am sure, do many of the players involved and the supporters who were fortunate enough to witness such a unique double. It just rained goals. We'd our reserve goalie playing, Anderson, that day and Hibs raced to a 4–0 lead. We pulled two back, Hibs made it 5–2, we pulled back all 3 goals and I got the equaliser. I remember Hibs goalie Allan tipped over a header which I thought had won it then we all thought Ian Hunter's shot had crossed the line. The Ref' said no and Hibs scored in the 90th minute - what a game! That season Mr Cunningham had brought in the brilliant uncompromising ex Hearts defender Roy Barry as we'd lost an unusually high number of goals in the previous season. Well, the Celtic game was the reverse.

We raced to a 4–2 lead soon after half-time and mine was a gift. A throw in came in across the box, no one challenged for it so I poked it home! Celtic pulled it all back and we lost again in the last minute. I have fond memories of a lot of good goals in my Dunfermline days but I think the most important came in the Cup in a 1–0 home victory against Killie. We'd played them at Rugby Park in January 1967 and I scored twice in a 2–2 draw. The day, of course, is now best remembered for the sensational goings on at Berwick! With Rangers out there was a great determination to do well in the replay and I scored the only goal. Martin hit a long ball up to wee Alex Edwards. He gave me a great ball and I slammed it into the right hand corner of the net. We put out Partick 5–1 in the next round but came to grief 1–0 at Tanadice in the Quarter-Final tie'. There was considerable interest in football in 1966, the appetite whetted by the World Cup that summer in England. In Europe Dunfermline beat Frigg of Oslo 3–1 to win 6–2 on aggregate with Alex scoring in Norway. 'By the time we'd the difficult tie with Dinamo Zagreb I was having constant troublesome knee injuries and we beat them 4–2 having, at one point been 1–2 down. Wee Alex had a blinder and scored from the spot after a defender handled my shot. I got 2 late goals to settle it. We went out on aggregate ironically due to the new away goals rule. Their first goal was yards offside too'! Dunfermline were having an unusually disappointing domestic season. They finished in 8th position despite Alex's 29 goals. Hughie Robertson was a long way back on 15.

Alex Ferguson – 'the happiest days of my playing career'

They had qualified for the League Cup Quarter-Final but lost by an astonishing aggregate of 4–9 to Celtic. In the league Alex scored a hat-trick in a 6–0 New Year pasting of Ayr United and he scored his last goals for the club on April 29th when he scored 2 penalties in a 4–0 home win over Falkirk on the day Foinavon won the Grand National at 100/1! Wherever the Pars played, Dunfermline's teenage element, in a huge away support, kept up the monotonous, not to say inane, chant of 'Fergie Fergie' and, in those far off days before the Criminal Justice Scotland Act, you risked a hail of beer cans descending on you, as happened to the writer on 18th February 1967 when Fergie scored the equaliser in a 1–1 Cup game at Partick! In the summer of 1967 George Farm became manager and, just 24 hours after he brought with him Pat Gardner from Raith Rovers, 'Scott Symon concluded the deal already set up with Mr Cunningham to take me to Ibrox for the then Scottish record fee of £60,000. Then Willie Callaghan and I were picked for the Scotland team which went on a World tour. It was an honour for me to bring Aberdeen to East End in 1985 on the occasion of the Centenary celebrations and meet up with Jock Stein and all my old mates. At a big club you do get an awful lot of invitations but there was never any doubt I would accept that one as I owed so much to the club as a player. I was delighted to see the revival which followed in the Leishman era because my 3 years were simply my best days as a player. It would be great to see the glory days return. Dunfermline are ambitious, they are back in the top league and it would be fantastic to see them get back into European football. I had such marvellous memories from the great European nights. At the end of last season as Manchester United were poised to win the Premiership, which I still regard as my greatest achievement, I just had to take time out to phone Bert to wish the team well. It was great both clubs did it together! The pressure on both of us, mainly from the media, had been enormous, but you have to cope'!

—8—

PAT GARDNER

More than a quarter of a century after Cup Final hero Pat Gardner left East End to go to Dundee United, at a real 'steal' at £5000, his name can still arouse debate among those who recall the late 1960s. He signed for £20,000 from Raith Rovers on 31st July 1967 'And I recall the club was congratulating itself on getting me for £40,000 less than the record fee received for Fergie, even though, at the time, £20,000 was a record fee for Dunfermline too. The problem was that, as I got to know my new colleagues and prepared for a friendly with Borussia Dortmund, the media were telling the fans I would be a direct replacement for Alex. I was a totally different player. He was lethal in the box. I made goals and tended to score from long distance'. 25 years on fans still discuss the value of his contribution. To some he was the man who, every bit as much as Roy Barry, won the Cup for the Pars. Others recall tearing their hair out at the open goals he missed from close range. 'Borussia included Held and Emmerich, who'd played one year earlier in the World Cup Final so re-emphasising the status of the club then. We lost 2–3. Dunfermline at first implemented the strict 4–2-4 system which Mr Farm had used to such great effect at Starks Park gaining promotion. I remember my first game. We drew 2–2 at Killie in the League Cup and I scored the first goal in Scotland for the season. Kerrigan took an Edwards pass deep into Killie's defence, squared it and I lashed it home from 18 yards then I got carried off! I came back a month later and enjoyed getting the winner in a 2–1 win at Raith in which Ian Lister played against us. A month later, I felt my honeymoon period had come to an end. We lost at home to our provincial rivals Killie 1–2 in the league and the papers blamed my lack of pace and concentration. Mind you, I was in good company. They blamed Bertie too! Overall, people now look back on it as a good

96

Many fans underestimated Pat's contribution to Dunfermline

season, for obvious reasons, but by year's end we kept being told that it had been the worst start since the late 1950s. The club had fallen well down the table so Mr Farm reverted to a 4-3-3 formation which concentrated more on defence and relied on fast breaks into attack. We didn't look back. It worked well and we took a point at Ibrox.

I felt things were beginning to click as we beat Morton 0–3 (A) and Partick Thistle 4–0 (H). All the criticism of us in the autumn was now stifled. It was at that time I remember Bertie's demolition of Raith at New Year in a 6–0 rout, one factor in all this being the remarkable play of Hughie Robertson as a link-man'. Dunfermline's hopes of a good run in the Cup seemed to receive a major set back when they were drawn to meet Celtic, then European Cup holders, at Parkhead in Round 3, the fourth time in 7 years they'd been drawn together. 'George Farm though was so determined to win. One week earlier, the team lost on BBC's 'Quiz Ball' with George Farm even complaining that Fulham had been prompted! The team contained Jim Fraser who was the brains of the outfit. Anyway, we went to Celtic off an excellent 4–2 home win over Aberdeen. We prepared at Dunblane and Mr Farm said 'play your normal game'. He told us all the strain is on Celtic, no one expects us to win anyway. He said we have lost the last 8 games against them but who hasn't? We knew that the crowd noise would spur Celtic on and it usually demoralised the opposition. The 1961 win was now very distant. The result there, which is now famous, was no fluke and Celtic lacked the flair that had won the European Cup. We were so determined to win and exploited all their weaknesses especially after Bertie Auld fouled Fraser.

I remember my goal well. Cattenach was short with a pass back challenged by Alex, I raced on to it, beat Ronnie Simpson and stroked it into the net. A home defeat 0–1 by Hibs was to bring us back to earth. We won the next cup game mid week at the death when Alex scored against the Dons' Clark, who'd defied us all evening. When we met Partick in the Quarter-Final, Roy Barry the 'anchor' of our team was suspended and the veteran Raith man Kinloch came in. He played in a 1–2 defeat by Rangers in which we were unlucky to lose and in the 1–0 Quarter-Final win over Partick Thistle! The defence saved us that day and Bertie and I just couldn't get past George Niven. I'd just missed a sitter when Bertie and I worked a one-two near the end and Bertie finished it. We were now favourites to win the Cup'. By now the *Dunfermline Press* was bemoaning the fact that, if the Pars played on Cup Final Day, then the crowd would be adversely affected by the Ibrox league game with Aberdeen that same day. 1968 was a different world. 'As we prepared for the match against St Johnstone in the Tynecastle Semi-Final Mr Farm had to warn us against over confidence. We had Jim Fraser and Roy Barry back and the club now had my old Raith mate Ian Lister. We were on a good run and the defence was tight. Maybe it was all about pride coming before a fall because about 8000 Pars fans travelled and we were awful. We were saved by the fact that, after the shock opener when Saints scored in a strong blustery wind, we knew their goalie was weak on his left foot. Bertie positioned himself on his right side, he cleared weakly and I only had to side foot it home from the penalty spot - so I did score from short range sometimes! I'd a header near the end that was touched over too. Mr Farm knew that we needed someone else up front and Ian was to hit a screamer from an Edward's cross to settle it in the mid-week replay. Saints were a well drilled team and I recall they scored first again. I made the equaliser for Bert and then we missed a penalty'. Dunfermline hit some dire form as they prepared for the Cup Final and to retain fourth in the table. They lost 0–2 to Airdrie thanks to Drew Jarvie and 2–1 to Stirling at Annfield. Mr Farm had to act and one week before the Cup Final Dunfermline won 1–2 at Partick Thistle and John McGarty replaced Jim Fraser in defence.

On 27th April 1968, Cup Final day duly arrived. Other entertainment then included the Kelty Musical Association performing 'Showboat' at the Carnegie Hall, the East Port Cinema was showing 'Bonnie and Clyde' (Admission 1/6) there were also films at the Palace and Regal, or on TV you could watch Des O'Connor, the Billy Cotton band show, or Dixon of Dock Green, Businesses took out advertising space to give public support to the Pars and Provost John Crawford (who claimed, later he'd left the date free in his diary since the previous August) prepared for the civic reception. Over 150 coaches travelled that day and a special train. 'The players were more confident and relaxed now as we prepared for the Final. This may seem ludicrous because our league form had been awful and we'd not played well in the previous 2 Cup games but Mr Farm reminded us we were a skilful team who had the edge over Hearts and he briefed us fully on the weaknesses we were to exploit. Of course, we had one major advantage. We had Roy Barry. They didn't.' Roy, perhaps the greatest cult hero of them all, post war, was signed from Hearts in the autumn of 1966. If Dunfermline's one major weakness of the mid-1960s was at the heart of the defence, then Mr Cunningham had just plugged it. He cost just £13,000 and went straight into the Athletic team which played Frigg in the Fairs Cup. He was to have many memorable games for the Pars including the West Brom and Slovan Bratislava European ones, in addition to the Cup Final. When he went to Cantwell's Coventry in October 1969 for £45,000, he claimed it was the ambition to play in the hardest league in the world. In reality he appeared to be a marked man as far as Scots Refs were concerned although he had little cause to moan the day he and John Lunn fell out in a league match and such were the remonstrations he was sent packing! 'With the presence of Roy Barry leading us we were bound to feel confident. Having beaten Dundee United 1–4 (A) had helped us too'.

Meanwhile, the ever loyal *Dunfermline Press* published a full page team photo (it did not include McGarty!) and a song sheet for the coach journey. As usual 'The Happy Wanderer' appeared along with versions of 'John Brown's Body', 'Clementine', 'Hello Dolly' etc. It was all far removed from 'Ghostbusters', 'Simply the Best' and 'Go West'. There was also a quiz covering everything from what was the largest gate (it was broken a week later) and the fastest goal? In the pen pics Pat was described as 'hard working, strong going, with a powerful shot'. In an editorial the paper wished Dunfermline had a player the calibre of Andy Wilson. In fairness, in their tribute to the team a week later, the *Press* wrote 'Gardner took pride of place on the big day. It was the first time he'd scored a brace and what a day to choose. Cruikshank probably didn't see either Gardner shot on the way in'! Pat recalls Hearts had to be treated with respect. 'We were 4th in the table, Hearts 12th but in the league they beat us 1–3 (H) and 2–1 (A). The one shock was the inclusion of John McGarty who played at no. 4. Jim Fraser, who'd fought back from injury, didn't make the bench. Hearts had Dunfermline's old star George Miller, Donald Ford up front and Cruikshank in goal and opted for the team which put out Morton in the Semi. Our team was: Bent Martin, W Callaghan and Lunn, McGarty, Barry, T Callaghan, Lister, Paton, Gardner, Robertson and Edwards. Sub: Thomson. It was 0–0 at half-time and there were few chances. I got in one header but that was all, but we were beginning to pull their defenders out of position. At half-time George Farm left us in no doubt that we'd not come all this way to lose and let rip at the two wingers. He told them get down the

Pat Gardner scores the opener in the 1968 Cup Final 3–1 over Hearts

And celebrations ensue

flanks and cross the ball to Bert and me. I'd great admiration for Mr Farm. Like any manager whose playing career was spent in goal he built his team around the defence. He always told us to play to our strengths. I remember the second half as if it were yesterday and I've played it on my video a thousand times. Cruikshank had some great saves at the start of the second period but then I got the breakthrough. Ian Lister swung in a free kick, the goalie pushed it out and I met it on the volley. I thought Bert was going to seal it minutes later when he got on the end of a superb Robertson pass but as he rounded the goalie he was brought down. Ian found the corner of the net with the penalty. We seemed to have done it but Hearts brought on the Scandinavian Moller and he hit an excellent cross which poor John Lunn put in his own net. Exactly 3 minutes later we wrapped it all up. Alex took a throw in, George Miller miscued it, Bert Paton got to it, turned it back and I think that was one of my best shots as it flew into the net!

You never forget a day like that; it was absolutely brilliant. Mr Farm had said from the outset we would win the Cup and he was vindicated'. 'As we returned to Dunfermline, I am sure the clock at the City chambers had been turned back seven years! Everything came to a halt in the High Street as the open top bus ran us to the council buildings to the tune of Cliff Richard's 'Congratulations' and about 25,000 cheering us. We all felt it made up for the awful disappointment of not having our lap of honour. We'd had a private meal in a Glasgow hotel and once we reached Kincardine, Fife Police escorted us all the way and every village we passed, people came out to cheer us. We all took turns at going out on the balcony and above us flew the club flag. The volume of noise for Mr Farm and then Roy Barry, who pretended he would climb over the balcony, was phenomenal. We watched the TV highlights and then shared some special cake with black and white icing and a few fans were still outside as we left to go home'. There was some disappointment that only 56,363 attended what was a memorable game but 27,816 and a lot more besides watched Pat Gardner score in the 1–2 defeat by league Champions Celtic the following Tuesday. At one point players were taken off and the game which was not all ticket was almost abandoned. 'I ended up with 16 goals to Bert's 18 in 1967–68.'

'I'll always remember 1968–69 for the European Cup Winners Cup run. I made 190 appearances in Pars colours and scored 55 goals but 5 of them were in my 14 European matches and the most crucial was against West Brom. The season got off to a good start as I got another brace in a 3–2 defeat of our bogey team United but we had been down 0–2. Playing Apoel Nicosa in Round 1 of Europe was a romp. We won 10–1 in the first leg and I got one. I remember Willie Callaghan got 2 and it seemed amazing the Cypriots scored. We'd lost at that time 3–1 at Hearts, but went on a good run after Cyprus and the aggregate was 12–1 in the end. By the November we knew Olympiakos would be tough in Round 2, their team was packed with Greek internationalists and Mr Farm emphasised we must get a decent lead in the first leg to take to Athens. It was a tough game, their manager said they would not lose it but we won 4–0 and silenced their noisy fans long before the end.

Their gamesmanship was awful. By the time we flew out, Bert was in hospital having been butted and punched and Mr Farm requested an official observer form UEFA as we'd had verbal threats against us! Well in the second leg the Ref let the game get out of hand, Barry Mitchell was sent off, the tackling was brutal and we were glad to survive 4–3 aggregate. At the end of the year I got my first hat-trick for the team in a 5–1 win demolition of Aberdeen but there was some disappointment when we got English representatives West Brom in the Quarter-Final as many had hoped it would be the Final'. Prices for the tie included 6/- for the ground and 20 shillings for the Centre Stand. Pat remained on form and scored 2 in a 6–2 rout of St Mirren just before Christmas and 2 at New Year in a 0–3 win at Raith. As West Brom approached the media regarded it as the Pars' hardest game since they met Valencia and all agreed on how crucial a home lead would be. 'They had Jeff Astle, of course, but also the likes of Wilson, Talbut and a young Asa Hartford. We put up a whirlwind start but could not get the breakthrough. I did some fast interpassing with Shug, Alex and Bertie but Osborne saved all we threw at him. In defence Fraser and Barry held firm and

Pat scores against West Bromwich Albion

Willie Duff had some great saves. By the time of the second leg I'd got one of my better goals in the Cup with a header from a John Lunn cross at Raith as we won 0–2. We then got a formidable game up at Pittodrie, a team whose record included 4 Cup Final appearances since the war. Mr Farm took us down to a hotel in Sutton Coldfield and he was still confident because the Midlands side would now have to come out and that would lead to gaps. I can think back to a bitterly cold night, a bone hard sanded pitch and a howling gale and about 2,000 Pars fans shouting themselves hoarse! Mr Farm's tactics were spot on. We were sound in defence and broke quickly into attack. In the opening minutes Alex Edwards took a pass from Paton and got fouled on the edge of the box. Alex took the kick himself, it was cleared, it rebounded to me and I placed my header past the sprawling goalie at the post. Roy Barry dictated play all evening and for the first time we were in the last 4 in Europe!' Despite a few snags 7,000 freezing fans watching screens at East End were in raptures too. Dunfermline drew 2–2 at Pittodrie but the Cup holders went out in the East End replay 0–2. So many games were now taking their toll. By the time Mr Farm witnessed the European Cup Winners Cup Semi-Final draw against Slovan Bratislava of Czechoslovakia, he'd spent a record £25,000 on former Rangers start George McLean and the Press was describing 'Fergie' as the 'forgotten man at Ibrox' where Colin Stein and Willie Johnston were now the main strike force. McLean scored immediately in a 2–2 draw at Aberdeen. Slovan came from what is now Slovakia, included 6 of the national team and had already disposed of Torino and Porto. As the Pars prepared for the game, Athletic fans had an outcry about ticket prices. 'He took us to Dunblane again and Bert and I were struggling to get fit. He told us they were a footballing side who rarely fouled and we'd the huge advantage of the home crowd. Our team was Duff, Callaghan and Lunn, Fraser, Barry and Renton: Robertson, Paton, Edwards, Gardner and Lister.

Slovan were a clever team who had splendid ball control and passing, and they came out of defence at speed but at half time Jim Fraser got the breakthrough. Alex took a free kick out on the right, Jim headed it on, then Bert pulled it back from the bye line and Jim finished the move. We threw everything at them near the end, they broke away and their no. 11 lobbed Duff. Mr Farm's attitude was that it wasn't over yet by any means. They would be no more difficult than West Brom. We went there hoping to be the first Scottish Provincial side to make the Final but their nippy winger Capkovic was to score the winner. I remember it because there was a huge crowd who cat called us all night, there was a strong wind, umpteen stoppages as the Ref could not control the game and I was sent off! I ended that season top scorer with 17 goals.' Dunfermline made a poor start to 1969–70, though Pat lashed home an excellent goal in the Pars second choice all blue strip when they defeated Celtic 2–1 in August. 'The following month I got another in the 4–0 win over Bordeaux and two of the Frenchmen were ordered off. Mr Farm warned us to be on our best behaviour in the second leg and not retaliate, the close marking of Alex in the first leg had been euphemistically robust! When we got to France we went down 2–0 but the local fans were wound up by some biased reports of the East End game and notably two of their favourites being sent off and we'd to show amazing restraint in the face of terrible provocation all evening. In the second round we met Gwardia of Warsaw. We were second in the league behind Hibs and Roy Barry had finally got his transfer. We were having some good results including 2–1 over Killie and Aberdeen but the Polish game was no classic. I got a late winner in the 2–1 match from yet another cross by Alex'. One funny aspect of this game was that local Polish war hero Mr Leszczuk senior was called in to help with the radio commentary. Unfortunately as he gallantly gave advice on the pronunciation of the Polish players names, no one thought to tell him which team was which and the Pars played in red. So every time Pat was on the ball Mr Leszczuk would whisper Dawiec Zynski and so it went on! 'We achieved our first ever win behind the Iron Curtain in that second leg wining 0–1. I got a pass to Billy Renton in the opening minutes and he set in one of his 30 yard rockets and, after that, we never looked back. We came straight back to a top of the table clash at Hibs and lost 3–0 mid-week. By the time we lost 1–0 to Anderlecht in the first leg of the Fairs Cup Round 3 we were all down that Bert's leg break meant he was out till the end of the season. Anderlecht were probably one of the most star studded teams to come to East End and we did well to beat them 3–2 though it was not enough. I little realised that match was the end of an era.

I remember it was about then that George Farm promised us yet another trip to Dunblane Hydro. Well there can't have been the cash because, at a subsequent team talk, he told the players it was off. George McLean told Farm 'you always go back on your word.' Mr Farm said 'I'll see you outside.' Suddenly the lights went out in the room. When they came back on, big George had disappeared! Soon after we lost to Celtic 2–1 in the Cup, captained by young McNicholl'.

As the team's form slumped in the months which followed, the team was heavily barracked by the fans and, in a poor home defeat by Morton, Mr Farm took Pat off because of the abuse he was taking. By the end of March he was so unhappy he asked away. Now and again Dunfermline could turn it on as in a 2–1 home win against Rangers in the March but ominously the second half of the season saw the poorest points haul in 7 years. They ended up with 35 points and in 9th place yet had had 22 points before Christmas. Things got no better at the beginning of 1970–71 and the Athletic were trounced 0–6 by Rangers. On 11th September half the 'Press' front page was devoted to Mr Farm's denial that he would resign. On October 2nd the same 'Press' front page announced that the Athletic, without a win in 14 games all season, had sacked him. Only a year earlier, the Board had fought to stop him moving to Ibrox. It was all to have a profound effect on Pat.

'Mr Farm had always rated me. I come from Coatbridge and he first signed me from Bellshill Athletic for Queen of the South, later he took me on at Starks Park'. Alex Wright became the new manager but the season was wretched with the club dodging relegation by a whisker.' Pat Gardner was equal top scorer with just 10 goals but that was 2 more than in 1970. 'It was an unhappy time. Jim Fraser and Willie Callaghan joined me in asking for a transfer. Bert Paton was getting over his bad injury, Doug Baillie was now a journalist, and Alex Edwards and Barry Mitchell didn't turn up for training. We looked forward to the new British Cup and a tie with Tottenham but were destroyed over 2 legs 0–7. Good results were few and far between though I scored in a 1–1 home draw with Rangers just after beating Arbroath in the Cup 3–1, a Joe McBride inspired Pars actually drew 1–1 in the Cup at Celtic Park but lost the home replay 0–1.' That summer the club plunged into financial crisis. 'Season 1971–72 saw the few remaining Cup players leave including Jim Thomson, Hughie Robertson, Alex Edwards and Bert Paton. In January 1972 I signed for Dundee United and I ended 1971–72 as their top goal scorer with 15 goals. I was to play in another Cup Final for them but we were heavily defeated 3–0 by Celtic. I moved on to Motherwell and got to another Cup Semi, finishing my career at Arbroath. I've spent the last 4 years coaching S form boys at Celtic and have really enjoyed it. Every Saturday though I look for the Pars score when the results come in. I enjoyed the Centenary celebrations and the 25th anniversary of the Cup win. They were great times and I retain huge affection for the club.'

—9—

CRAIG ROBERTSON

O f the Championship match on 4th May, award winning sports writer Graham Spiers wrote in *Scotland On Sunday*, 'Dunfermline are up. The very words almost have the force of a release from a prison sentence. They're up, and the news is sweeter in that they are promoted as First Division champions. Around East End Park yesterday, amid loud music, blazing sunshine and a good hour of dreadful nerves, these facts were finally, joyously proclaimed'. Spiers captured the mood superbly. One could almost reach out and touch the relief that day. The Pars huge support and the local population had craved the Championship flag more than anything for 4 desperately long years, not just for its own sake but because it was the key which would unlock the door to Aladdin's cave. The burden of expec-

Craig celebrates his goal against Raith Rovers in August 1988

tation for months had rested on one man's shoulders more than any other, 33 year old captain Craig Robertson. He knew, full well, that, at the time of the tragedy in January, many felt the Athletic's Championship Challenge would fold. 'It would have been easy, after Norrie's death, for us to think our season was finished but we didn't, and that's to the credit of the boys. This was the greatest day, beyond doubt, in my whole football career. I am lucky enough to be the skipper of the team in the Champions' dressing room and I'll never forget today. I have been through every emotion both in today's match with Airdrie, and during the season generally'. Craig Robertson had been inspirational all season and is an enthusiast who leads from the front. Appointed player-coach in 1996–97, many feel he may, in years to come, be Dunfermline manager, but he had difficulty becoming the Captain in such desperate circumstances and, while the Scottish Football League insisted the Athletic return to using a no. 4 jersey from August '96, Craig made it clear that, he personally, would not want to put it on.

To become captain of a team for which you profess both loyalty and affection is normally a tremendous honour but, in January 1996, it put an immense strain on Craig. He was as devastated as anyone else. However, he was utterly determined to win the flag for Norrie. 'The players were torn apart at the news and suddenly the Clydebank game was the most difficult of our lives. The dressing room was so silent for days. You just sat there waiting for him to walk in . You didn't dare mess with him as he always got the last laugh. Norrie was actually a very private guy, he didn't have a close friend in the team, his great pal was former Pars star John Watson. The greatest tribute to him was now obvious but it was going to be extremely difficult to achieve. In the meantime, I knew I would be overwhelmed as we came out before the fans at that first game but we had to be professional and get on with it. The longer we stayed off, the harder it was going to get'. When the match did come, it was punctuated by long periods of numbing silence and Dick Campbell repeatedly sent out the subs to cheer on the crowd. When Clydebank pulled back all three goals on that bitterly cold January afternoon there was still an irrational feeling, many fans have remarked on since, that it would all come good in the end. With minutes to go, there was a colossal thunderbolt shot by Craig which slammed off a post and bulged the net. Graham Spiers wrote 'To the outsider, there was a warming symbolism about Robertson scoring the goal. Like McCathie, this fellow has been a talisman down the years, scoring his barnstorming goals in his early years, disappearing off to Aberdeen, then returning to East End Park, never having left their affections in the first place. The way he seized the ball here in the 85th minute and utterly bashed it home made you realise again the restorative powers of football'. Craig added 'People might have thought it was a bit callous for us to play, but we wanted to do it for Norrie: it was what he would have wanted. I'm just glad today's over. I had tears in my eyes at the minutes' silence. We were drained during the match, the emotions of the week had taken their toll. I still don't know where that winning goal came from'.

Craig Robertson came to East End Park in May 1987 from Raith Rovers, where he'd played for six seasons scoring 23 goals, 13 of them in a great run in 1984–85. The fee was just £25,000. Initially he was only at East End for 18 months and Jim Leishman recalls 'My Board were not totally convinced but I had to hand it to them for their faith in my judgement. They just said you are in charge and they to their credit, did not interfere. They let me stand or fall by my record. Craig was one of the nicest players I ever met. He was a tremendous threat in midfield and had a knack of ghosting into the box like a Martin Peters. He made 63 appearances in a black and white jersey then and scored 19 goals in that spell. However, what gave us so much pride in the 1987–88 Premier season was that he would end up as the highest midfield scorer in the division yet, as a team, we'd been struggling. It spoke volumes for him to end up ahead of eg Paul McStay. Eventually, having knocked back so many clubs, Aberdeen, a top club with European ambitions, came for him and so he went to Pittodrie for £175,000. I fought really hard to keep him but at Aberdeen he was to score within 20 minutes of his debut and he'd also score in both the UEFA and Cup Winners Cup games'. Craig remembers 'I was glad to end up at a major club like Aberdeen. People tend to forget just how big a club like

Dunfermline are and frankly only Celtic, Rangers or the Dons would have attracted me away. However, Leishman had explained to me that the club was under pressure from the bankers (much as they were in 1995 with McNamara) to sell a player and I would attract £200,000. I'd scored against Queen of the South and then got injured just before this, then I got tonsilitis and I was in such a bad way that Pip Yeates, the physio who would go with Scotland to Euro '96, had me doing 'pre-season training' when I was asked to meet Tony Fitzpatrick. Dundee were also after me but I wasn't interested in going to a smaller club. As Jim drove me reluctantly to Love Street, Paisley, the mobile phone went. Aberdeen had come in for me. It was no contest. On the evening of Alex McLeish's testimonial, Jim drove me to Pittodrie and I signed for Alex Smith the following morning'.

Craig came from Dunfermline and, as a kid, went to the big games at East End, yet he was once part of that dying breed, a Cowdenbeath fan. 'I even remember one match which was delayed due to the size of the crowd — honest'! He went to Beath High School 'long after Jim Leishman was there', won Scottish boys club caps and was signed by Hearts in the Willie Ormond days but, in August 1980, Gordon Wallace took him to Starks Park. He was a key player for Raith playing midfield or in the sweeper role and destroyed the Pars, of all teams, in a thrilling 2–3 defeat at East End with a cracker of a goal which effectively ended the Athletic's promotion ambitions in 1984–85. People were sitting up and taking notice. 'Raith had an incredible end to that season and our shock 2–3 win at East End was only one of a 9 wins in a row spell which was a record for the Kirkcaldy club. Bobby Wilson, the manager, would say to us, if you win today there's no training till the next game and so it went on till I think we lost our last game. He was a real psychologist was Bobby'! Craig was versatile, had tremendous work rate, good vision and a tremendously powerful shot. When Dunfermline finally came for him he had to contend with the difficult jump of 2 divisions. 'I signed for Dunfermline because, although Raith had won promotion I felt I badly needed a change after 6 years and I saw the Athletic as a big, full-time ambitious club. In addition, Jim and I went back a long way. The first competitive game I ever played in was a wolf cub match and Jim refereed it in Cowdenbeath! Dunfermline were up to the Premier on the same day that Raith got promoted to Division 1 and personally I was so ambitious. I'd also played with John Watson and Norrie McCathie in the Scottish Semi-Professional team. I found the Premier so much quicker and competitive and it took a while to adjust. I'd learned a lot from my different managers and the experienced players I'd played alongside and I now wanted to put that to good effect. I didn't have a favourite position. All I wanted was success for the club and myself - I'd have played in goal if asked'! It was not only Craig who had to adjust. The Pars had raced from Division 2 to Division 1 to the more rarified atmosphere of the Premier 1986–88 and now there was the immediate realisation that Dunfermline had to compete with teams who could rely on monopoly money.

Jim Leishman snapped up Craig along with Graeme Robertson (Queen of the South), George Cowie (Hearts), Stuart Beedie (Hibs) and, once Ian McCall was transferred to Rangers for £200,000, Craig found himself alongside what Leishman called 'The four Kings for whom I'd sold my ace' ie Mark Smith (Celtic), Billy Kirkwood (Dundee United), John Holt (Dundee United) and Gary Riddell (Aberdeen). Leishman knew full well that many of the players, who'd come up from Division 2, were not going to cope at this level. In 1987–88 he was to make 47 appearances and score 13 goals. One early match really stood out. On August 22nd, 18,070 saw the Pars beat Celtic 2–1 at home. Dunfermline were hardly expected to play with such skill and organisation but the Pars had come 'to bury Caesar not to praise him'. Goals by Craig and Eric Ferguson and a breathtaking display by Ian Westwater kept the bhoys at bay. Billy McNeill later commented 'I don't want to take anything away from Dunfermline but Celtic should have won'. 'Well, he was right. He didn't take anything away from Dunfermline'! When Ferguson and Craig Robertson each grabbed a brace in a 4–1 win over Morton though, the points frankly were all the more valuable. 'The players knew full well we were battling in a mini-league against Motherwell, St Mirren, Falkirk and Morton.

Craig challenges the goalkeeper, watched by Gary Riddell, in a fixture
against St. Johnstone

There could only be the one life belt'. As the season ended,
Dunfermline crushed Dundee 6–1, Morton 3–0, beat St Mirren
2–1, held Aberdeen 1–1 and, of course, put Rangers out of the
Cup 2–0 and one was left with the distinct impression that,
having completed a period of transition, the team had simply run
out of games. Craig scored his 13th with a superbly placed 25
yarder against St Mirren in mid-April. 'The season certainly
whetted the appetite for the top league. Memories of defeats soon
dim but the size of the gates, the frequent appearances of the
cameras, and the sight of so many internationalists who were
household names gracing the East End turf stayed with you for
a long time.

I will never forget either our final match at Celtic Park when
it was Celtic's centenary. Long after the game ended and we were
all sitting in the dressing room, a police sergeant came in and

said, if you don't come out and take a bow before your fans, we will never get them to go home. The supporters were brilliant.' Two other goals by Craig Robertson that season certainly merit a mention. He scored a brilliant equaliser in the 3–2 defeat by Hearts and maybe the best worked when he scored with his familiar rocket shot against Hibernian at home after a brilliant run and cross by Beedie in a match in which Smith and Beedie had tormented Hibs on both flanks. 'Stuart Beedie made most of my goals that season, Billy Kirkwood and John Holt were a great help to me that season and I learnt a great deal from the three of them about what it takes to be a full-time pro.' He has other memories of that season too. 'I learned, not surprisingly, that Ibrox was unlike any other ground in Scotland for its unique atmosphere. And the impact of the huge Pars support in so many games was crucial to us. As we began the season 1988–89 that huge support and our good players combined to make us the Rangers of the first division. In short, every team would raise their game against us. In some away grounds, there was a problem with the lack of atmosphere. However the Pars support was so large and vocal at little away grounds you could be forgiven for feeling you were playing at home'. When Craig left Dunfermline in December 1988 he'd already scored 5 goals in 16 appearances. One was vital in the 2–1 home defeat of his former club Raith.

There were mixed emotions at him leaving, namely delight that his talents had been recognised by a top club but regret that the Athletic's task would now be all the harder. Craig, who as a child wanted to be a fireman, did not really set the heather on fire up at Pittodrie. 'I was confined mainly to Aberdeen reserves but made 15 appearances scoring 4 times for them in the league. My biggest disappointment was missing out on the Skol Cup Final for Aberdeen against Rangers when the Dons won after extra time. I still regret the fact that I feel I did not get a fair crack of the whip. I can still look back at one of the greatest goals I ever scored against Rapid Vienna and I also got one against Apoel Nicosia. In the Austrian game, Theo Snelders threw the ball out to Willie Miller on the edge of the penalty box, he passed it on to Jim Bett who played a fifty yard pass into my path and

I met it on the volley and crashed it home. However in league games I think I must have set some sort of record for coming on as sub. Aberdeen had a set formation which they stuck with week after week and they tended to bring me on only if they were losing. I liked to get forward from midfield but that was not the role I was given. However, being there was a great learning process. It gave me an insight into how a big club is run and what I learned I now use when I coach young players today. There were happy moments too. I made great friends there like Willie Miller - who I have learned so much from - Claire his wife and their two kids Mark and Victoria and I also met my wife Laura up there.' In August 1991 Iain Munro brought him back to East End for £100,000. 'Dunfermline had such a pull for me. I knew other clubs were in for me but I wanted to get back to East End.

I was taken aback at the contrast in atmosphere at the club in such a short space of time'. Munro had kept the club out of danger in 1990–91 finishing on 27 points but crowds had fallen to an average 8,257. As the season got under way he spoke of his optimism for the new season but called for everyone, including players and fans, to pull together. His optimism was misplaced. Dunfermline remained a desperately unhappy club and would finish the season with an abysmal collection of 18 points and just 4 wins. One of the few highlights though was Craig's return and he showed why he was in such demand with a superbly headed goal against Dundee United, yet he would score only 2 all season.

Against the backdrop of a disastrous start to the league campaign, Dunfermline, a club which has rarely done much in the League Cup in their history, contrived to reach the Final. There was an easy enough gentle start in Round 2 of the Skol Cup as they dismissed Alloa 4–1 but the tempo increased in Round 3 as they put out St Mirren in a penalty shoot out after a 1–1 draw. Craig's vital goal came on September 3rd when 7,220 saw Dunfermline upset the form book in beating much fancied Dundee United, yet in the league just 4 days later the hapless Pars would lose 3–0 at Tannadice. 10,662 attended the Semi-Final at Tynecastle, where the Athletic were awarded 'that penalty' in the dying minutes and then progressed on a penalty

Note the determination of Craig Robertson in action

shoot out to Hampden. On 27th October, before 40,377, Dunfermline went down 0–2 to Hibernian, by which time Iain Munro was gone. The thought occurred that many more outstanding Dunfermline Athletic teams had never reached the Cup Final yet this one was, at best, ordinary. New manager Jocky Scott knew 1992–93 would be extremely difficult in competition with the likes of Raith Rovers and Kilmarnock, who were to end up in the top 2 positions come May. Craig Robertson had earlier taken considerable stick from the fans in 1992 because, having languished for so long in a reserve team, they felt he was carrying too much weight and had lost some of his pace and sharpness. 'Actually I felt much of that criticism was so unfair. The fans did not seem to understand that Jocky Scott told me to sit in front of the back 4 and protect them and let Billy Davies go forward but that really isn't the role I am comfortable with'. Craig was leaner and fitter in the new season having gained from pre-season training but even so took only 3 goals from 38 appearances. In a season in which they took 15, 11 and 18 points in the first three quarters they amassed only 8 to throw it all away and the folklore of the Pars bottling it at the death, so beloved by the West of

Scotland's tabloids, was born. The season ended with the humiliating defeat by Cowdenbeath at home and the public apology
by Jocky Scott who got embroiled in heated words with the fans.

In August 1993 Bert Paton was in post. It was to be a
memorable season as the crowds were attracted again by the
attractive brand of attacking football he encouraged and, after
a period of instability even Chairman Roy Woodrow felt moved
to comment that there was now a 'highly skilled and dedicated
staff throughout the club'. Dunfermline missed out by 1 point as
runners up to Falkirk. Craig had an excellent season scoring 4
goals in 40 appearances. 'Fifers are a strange lot. They like their
own folk. In Bert Paton the club appointed a quiet man who is
one of the nicest guys I have ever met in the game. He can put
his point over when he needs to and he hates to lose. He knows
players' strengths and encourages you to play your normal game
and to express yourself. When he came to East End, the atmosphere changed completely. I really enjoyed playing beside Paul
Smith. He and I had this daft superstition that if we were on a
good run we'd wear the same underpants until we got beaten
again. Yes they were clean! It was sad that we lost our opening
games despite playing well, because we put so much into that
season but just couldn't make up for the poor start.' The desire
to see the club playing on a higher plane was exemplified by an
attendance of 13,357 when they met Falkirk in the 1–1 home
draw. 'The cruel 1–0 defeat at Broomfield finally did for us that
year' says Craig with feeling. 'In the last game George O'Boyle
hit 4 in the 5–0 pasting of Clyde but it was all too late and all
the players were moved by the reception of the fans in that final
game'. By 1994–95 the Pars fans knew they were now seeing
Craig at his peak and there was considerable relief when he
signed a new deal.

It was then that Craig went public on his views on league
reconstruction, articulating the view of so many players, managers and fans. 'It would be much better if we'd a Premier
division of say 16 clubs giving a healthier more competitive
variation to our Premier teams. There's too much hustle and
bustle, no room for adaptability and no room to groom individual players and bring on the younger ones. We should be

breeding players and not suppressing them out of fear and insecurity. Much of the fear stems from two of the clubs having to be relegated so over half the league is threatened. Even the coming of three points for a win has not changed much because some Division 1 teams still play a tight defensive game and then attack you on the break'. He also added that there would be a lot more fun in football if Refs had a bit of a laugh and a joke with players in a game as they used to instead of always being rigid in their interpretation of the rules. Craig feels strongly that it is vital that football is 'sold to the public in a positive manner and if a Ref was allowed to go public at the end of a match to explain some controversial decision, that would certainly contribute'. In 1993–94 Craig was none too concerned that he'd scored few goals. His own performances had been good 'and all that concerned me was the performance of the team. It did not matter who scored'. 1994–95 was the third consecutive year of disappointment, this time the club being pipped by Raith Rovers by 1 point. 'We drew too many away games it is as simple as that'. Craig made 45 appearances and took his goal scoring to 8. With Hamish French and Kenny Ward badly injured, Stewart Petrie unable to add to his handsome total of 21 goals in the run in, and newly signed Greg Shaw not even breaking his duck, manager Paton was relieved that 5 of them came in the last few weeks from the player who had made the no. 8 jersey his own and who controlled the midfield in every game he played. He was simply playing as well as he had back in 1987–88 when the talent scouts packed the stand. 'I actually had a bet on with Paul, Norrie and Andy as to who would get the most goals in those last few games and I won it!' No game better exemplified this than the play off first leg at Pittodrie. In years to come fans will probably look back on the incident when Ref Les Mottram's generosity saved Aberdeen's bacon as McKimmie pulled Moore down and it seemed a clear cut penalty to all but Les but, before that, Craig had brilliantly headed an Allan Moore corner past the Dons defence for the equaliser before later splitting the Dons defence with the long ball which led to Moore being toppled.

As season 1995–96 began Chairman Roy Woodrow expressed his frustration at seeing Kilmarnock, Falkirk and Raith Rovers getting established in the Premier Division while Raith had done so outstandingly well to win the Skol Cup and qualify for Europe, yet Dunfermline seemed destined to always miss out. He made yet another appeal for the football authorities to reconstruct the leagues now that top division 1 teams were clearly as good as most of their Premier counterparts. He thanked the huge support for being 'the extra man' and thanked the management team, who'd achieved so much against a back drop of financial limitations. They had re-established a mood of optimism at East End. In 1995–96 those limitations would lead to the unavoidable transfer of Jackie McNamara to give the club some financial breathing space.

'It was a blow to lose Jackie. He is a class player and he would have been a loss to any club'. In 1995–96 Craig was to make 32 appearances and score 5 goals including one in the crucial 4–1 home rout of challengers Morton in March. One of his best performances was in the sensational 0–1 win over Dundee United at Tannadice in the penultimate game. Paton said 'I thought all the boys were magnificent that day but, although I rarely single out players, I must say Craig was brilliant. On the Monday before the game he twisted his ankle and couldn't even train until the Friday but Craig was utterly determined to play and turned in a stunning performance'. 'As we went to Tannadice, where the team had not won since the same day in 1974, we knew that it was the 'winner takes all'. Whoever won that game would be Champions.

We'd been getting slagged by the West of Scotland's media ever since the autumn defeat up at Tannadice on a day when we'd seven of the first team players out. We'd been told we'd been journey men up against a class team of professionals and the flag was destined to go to Dundee United'. All season Bert had got the blend right using the experienced players like Robertson, Millar, Petrie, Moore, French, Smith, Den Bieman, Miller, Westwater, Van de Kamp etc beside the younger school of McNamara, Fleming, Tod, Ireland and Bingham and for the final couple of games he knew that the experience of the older players would be a crucial factor. In the run in the Athletic took 16 points but the crucial 3 would come at Tannadice. In that second last game, Dundee United's players appeared overwhelmed by the occasion yet the Athletic players looked confident from the off. Paton knew that if his players were patient against Airdrie on 4th May and the fans got behind them and they did not get involved in 'a cavalry charge', then all would come good in the end and so it proved. The team was: Westwater, Miller, Millar, Den Bieman, Tod, Fleming, Moore, Robertson, Smith, French and Rice. Subs: Shaw, Hegarty and Van de Kamp.

Craig gave a captain's performance, shouting, cajoling and encouraging the players around him and when everyone's hearts sank at the Airdrie equaliser, Craig led them on with new determination to ultimate victory and no one there that day will forget the sight of Craig and Andy Tod doing their victory jig in the centre circle as news came through that it was 2–2 at Cappielow. 'We were certainly inspired by the *Sun* on the Saturday at Tannadice when they came out with the famous 8–0 headline ie every other Division 1 manager was asked who'd win at Tannadice and everyone wrote us off. Then we had papers saying we were a team of giants (e.g. myself or Allan Moore?) who depended on the long ball game yet United humped the ball at us all afternoon. As for the usual comment about bottle, the only one we saw contained champagne on the final day'! At the time of the awful and inexplicable 1–3 defeat by Hamilton while most of the media and some Pars fans wrote the Athletic off, Kevin McCarra wrote in *The Sunday Times* 'Dunfermline will remain a fine old institution from a community where football is still entangled with life and, whether they succeed or not in the next few weeks, the club deserves only respect'. Craig Robertson's leadership, commitment and enthusiasm had brought back respect to the club as he led them back to the top of Scottish football. 'I'll never forget May 4th. The volume of noise from the 13,000 crowd was even louder than the din our fans had made at Tannadice. At that game United put their fans behind both goals to help encourage their team to the flag yet our fans outshouted them. I just felt that Dundee United would have to really fight if they were to take anything because I have seldom seen the Athletic look so psyched up. We pulled it off despite playing with 10 men for half an hour. It was surely pre-ordained that we should meet Airdrie in the last game. We'd always met them in the run-in and having drawn and lost the previous 2 years, I told the players we were due our win. The fans expected so much but I knew full well Airdrie would not lie down. There are many times in a Championship season when you can't play silky football, you must simply grind out results. The match was no classic but at least we came on to our best game after they equalised. After that euphoric moment, with 12 minutes to go, when we learned it was a draw at Morton and we were champions, I was so determined that we were not going to draw. I wanted that 4 point cushion after all the media had said. I couldn't believe how long we'd sit in the dressing room till the Cup arrived. I was totally drained. Holding the Trophy was an incredibly emotional moment especially as I felt like a burst balloon in the preceding three-quarters of an hour waiting. The celebrations that evening were wonderful'. It had been a long hard 4 years. As he sat in his victorous Championship top, clutching the champagne that Saturday afternoon, he said 'don't ask me yet about how we'll do in the Premier. Just allow us to savour this moment first. For us to stay up in 1996–97 will equal anything we have done this season, but on 4th May it's all a long way away. As captain, I will continue to push the players around me to give 110% – that way we should get at least 100% You see, winning isn't everything – it's the only thing'!

POSTSCRIPT

Dunfermline Athletic's Board and Chairman Roy Woodrow have ambitious plans for the club as they approach the millennium. Roy Woodrow has three main aims. First he wants to see the club consolidating their position in the Premier Division, a situation which would be made all the easier if the division were extended to 14 or 16 teams. Second he looks forward to the day when the Athletic returns to playing in Europe. Finally, he wants to see Dunfermline on a sound financial footing. 'There will be many people reading this book who will not have seen Paton, Smith, Fergie, or Edwards playing in a Pars strip or the team playing in Europe. Youngsters have no idea just how big a club we were in the 1960s and this then was one of the best stadia in Scotland. 5 years hence I want to see a compact all seated stadium at East End with the latest floodlighting. There will be more facilities here for other sports too. Today folk are more affluent and there's more leisure time and such a redevelopment would advance our position at the heart of our community. Today football is far more of a business than it was in the 1960s and we must attract more sponsorship and corporate hospitality etc. We have restructured this club in terms of the original debt. Dunfermline Athletic sold East End and Eagle Glen Training HQ to Dunfermline Sports Ground Ltd, so it can use its income from gate receipts and commercial ventures solely for football activities. That has made it easier for the club to meet the requirements of the Taylor Report. This will ensure the future of the club but we will never lose sight of the fact that the most important people at East End are the supporters. By that I mean the ones who support us week in and week out, through thick and thin, not the few whose support is conditional'.

In *Black and White Magic* (1984) Jock Stein said that, 'because of the way the game is shaped now, perhaps Dunfermline cannot return to the heights of the 1960s'. In 1996 Stuart McCall (Rangers) said 'that today only Celtic and perhaps Aberdeen or Hearts can really mount a challenge to the Ibrox club'. However, there's no reason why Dunfermline cannot get re-established in the Premier Division and return to Europe or win the Cup. If you never have a dream; how can you tell when a dream comes true?